Britannia AD 43–105

COMBAT

British Celtic Warrior

VERSUS

Roman Soldier

William Horsted

Illustrated by Adam Hook

OSPREY PUBLISHING
Bloomsbury Publishing Plc
Kemp House, Chawley Park, Cumnor Hill, Oxford OX2 9PH, UK
29 Earlsfort Terrace, Dublin 2, Ireland
1385 Broadway, 5th Floor, New York, NY 10018, USA
E-mail: info@ospreypublishing.com
www.ospreypublishing.com

OSPREY is a trademark of Osprey Publishing Ltd

First published in Great Britain in 2022

A catalogue record for this book is available from the British Library.

ISBN: PB 9781472850898; eBook 9781472850867;
ePDF 9781472850850; XML 9781472850836

22 23 24 25 26   10 9 8 7 6 5 4 3 2 1

Maps by www.bounford.com
Index by Rob Munro
Typeset by PDQ Digital Media Solutions, Bungay, UK
Printed and bound in India by Replika Press Private Ltd.

Osprey Publishing supports the Woodland Trust, the UK's leading
woodland conservation charity.

To find out more about our authors and books visit
www.ospreypublishing.com. Here you will find extracts, author
interviews, details of forthcoming events and the option to sign up for
our newsletter.

Artist's note

Readers may care to note that the original paintings from which the
colour plates in this book were prepared are available for private sale.
All reproduction copyright whatsoever is retained by the publishers. All
enquiries should be addressed to:

scorpiopaintings@btinternet.com

The publishers regret that they can enter into no correspondence upon
this matter.

CONTENTS

Introduction

Reverse of a coin of the Catuvellauni tribe displaying a mounted warrior carrying a *carnyx*. The Catuvellauni occupied an area of south-eastern Britain north of the River Thames in the 1st century AD, and led the resistance to the Roman invasion in AD 43. (Werner Forman/Universal Images Group/Getty Images)

OPPOSITE
A 1st-century AD relief showing two Roman soldiers, from a Roman building in Mainz, Germany, now in the Landesmuseum, Mainz. The figure on the left is wearing a *lorica segmentata*, and is carrying a *pilum* and a semi-cylindrical shield, or *scutum*, so is probably a legionary. (DeAgostini/Getty Images)

The Romans invaded Britain in the spring of AD 43 at the command of the emperor Claudius (r. AD 41–54). Roman involvement with the tribes of the south-east of Britain had steadily increased since Julius Caesar's expeditions to the island in 55 and 54 BC. Successive emperors had been keen to offer diplomatic and economic support to friendly tribal chieftains in return for access to Britain's mineral resources, in particular iron and silver. In the early 1st century AD, the most powerful ruler was Cunobeline, king of the Catuvellauni, whose territory roughly corresponded with the modern-day English counties of Hertfordshire and Essex. During his long reign, Cunobeline carefully managed to court Roman patronage without alienating those who feared Roman influence. Sometime in the early AD 40s, however, Cunobeline either died or became seriously ill. Two of his sons, Togodumnus and Caratacus, seized control and quickly moved against pro-Roman factions. They first ousted another brother, Adminius, who ruled a small territory in the north-east tip of what is now Kent; he fled to Claudius' predecessor Caligula (r. AD 37–41), whose planned invasion never materialized. Soon after, the anti-Roman brothers deposed Verica, the chieftain of the Atrebates, whose power was centred around Calleva (modern-day Silchester). Verica left Britain and appealed to Claudius for help.

Claudius agreed to send an expedition to Britain, with the invasion force commanded by Aulus Plautius. The Roman Empire at the time enjoyed a period of relative peace, so Plautius was able to gather an army of considerable strength from across Roman-controlled territory. At its core were four legions, providing 20,000 highly trained and well-equipped heavy-infantry soldiers, reinforced with artillery. Plautius probably also assembled at least as many auxiliary infantry and cavalry troops, again from all over the Roman Empire, including a number of cohorts of Batavians from the Rhine delta, and cavalry *alae* (sing. *ala*; literally 'wing', an all-mounted cavalry unit) from Thrace (Webster 1980: 85–87).

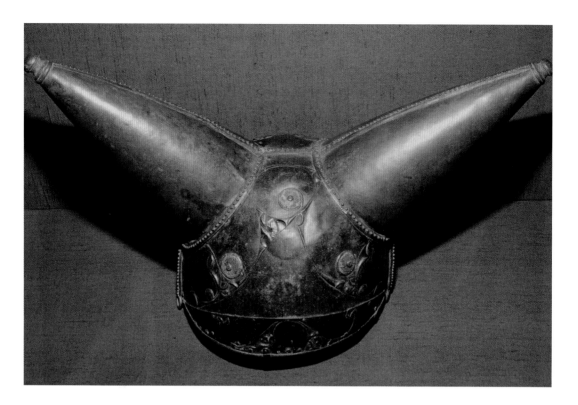

The famous 'Waterloo Helmet' (150–50 BC) was dredged from the River Thames near Waterloo Bridge in the early 1860s and shows the very high quality of metalwork produced by the British Celts. The 'horned' design is unique: no other Iron Age helmet with horns has yet been found in Europe. This was almost certainly a helmet produced for ritual or parade rather than battle: the 'horns' would have caught, rather than deflected, edged weapons, and it would have been cumbersome to wear. Although it was almost certainly deposited in the Thames for some religious reason, it was probably not made for this purpose; one of the horns has broken at some point and a replacement fitted. (CM Dixon/Print Collector/Getty Images)

We only have one literary source for the invasion of Britain: the brief account of Cassius Dio, a Roman statesman and historian originally from Bithynia in Asia Minor, who wrote a vast history of the Roman Empire in Greek. Dio records (*Roman History* 60.19–22) that the Roman army landed in Britain unopposed (probably at Richborough in Kent) because the British tribes were not expecting them. When the British did gather together into an army, they immediately adopted the strategy that would prove so successful against Roman commanders in Britain for centuries: they fell back into the marshes and forests, drawing the Roman force into terrain where the heavily equipped legionaries were unable to fight effectively, and refusing to meet the Romans in pitched battle. Plautius eventually managed to catch up with a British army commanded by Caratacus, whom he defeated, and then another led by his brother Togodumnus, who was killed. Plautius then followed the retreating Britons westward across Kent, finding them again on the far bank of the River Medway. The British appear to have assumed the Roman army could not cross the river without building bridges and took few precautions. They had not heard of the special skills of Plautius' Batavian auxiliary cavalry, however, who swam across the wide river alongside their horses and caught the British by surprise. More Roman troops led by the future emperor Vespasian also managed to ford the river and after two days of brutal fighting the Romans forced the British to flee once more, this time to the mouth of the River Thames.

Again, the British looked to the landscape to aid them, and slipped across the treacherous tidal flats of the Thames estuary, hoping to trap the Romans in the rising flood. After some confusion due to their ignorance of the terrain, the Batavians managed to cross, and other units found a bridge

further upstream. The Romans surrounded the Britons and killed many. The survivors melted away, luring a number of Roman soldiers to their deaths in the marshes.

Plautius consolidated his gains and set up garrisons in the territory he had conquered. He gathered the remainder of his army north of the Thames, ready to march on Cunobeline's capital at Camulodunum (modern-day Colchester). Here, however, Plautius was forced to stop, being under strict orders from Claudius to await his arrival in Britain before taking the enemy capital. Caratacus took immediate advantage of Plautius' delay, and retreated with his family and a force of loyal retainers further to the west, into the territories of other tribes, whom he persuaded to join his resistance. Plautius' failure to catch Caratacus was costly: the British leader would continue his guerrilla campaign for seven bloody years before his defeat and capture.

When Claudius arrived in the autumn of AD 43, he took command of his army and easily captured Camulodunum. He accepted the capitulation of several tribal leaders, and negotiated settlements with others. Claudius attempted to reinforce the borders of the new province of Britannia through treaties with friendly tribal leaders (Webster 1981: 13). It was common Roman practice to enlist the help of 'client kings' to administer newly conquered territory, which helped to reduce the burden on the army for peacekeeping duties, and provided a 'buffer zone' on the frontiers. The 'buffer zone' to the

We have little literary evidence for life in Iron Age Britain before the arrival of the Romans. The eminent archaeologist Barry Cunliffe posits (1997: 156–64) that archaeological analysis of settlement patterns and the distribution of pottery, weapons and other goods shows that Iron Age Britain was roughly divided into four different communities.

In the far south-western peninsula, and the south of what is now Wales, most people lived in fortified enclosures, large enough to contain a single extended family and their livestock, or easily defensible 'cliff castles' in coastal areas. Metal production was important to the economy of this region.

The south-east and east were dominated by tribes whose much larger, open settlements, and complex, hierarchical society, based around a powerful 'warrior elite', were very similar to those of neighbouring areas of what are now northern France and Belgium. Metalworking techniques and artistic styles spread here from across the Channel. It is in this part of Britain that most of the examples of beautifully decorated metalwork have been found, such as the so-called 'Witham' and 'Battersea' shields. Burial culture, particularly the practice of interring warriors with their two-wheeled chariots and other possessions, also mirrored that of the nearby European mainland.

Between the very different communities of the east and south-west, there was a large 'border' region, spreading northwards in a narrowing band from the central–southern coast to what is now north Wales. Although the cultures of the communities of this region differed in many respects, their landscapes and societies were dominated by the widespread construction of hillforts: large, fortified settlements built on the top of high hills, which could house a number of families and their animals in times of danger.

The fourth cultural group inhabited a region that extended around the north and west coast of Scotland and the Scottish Islands, where the people built massive stone settlements called 'brochs' or 'duns'. This community was isolated from much of the rest of Britain.

In the century before Julius Caesar's expeditions to Britain in 55 and 54 BC, there appear to have been several migrations of people from what are now northern France and Belgium into south-eastern Britain. The tribes of the areas in which they settled adopted many of the immigrants' cultural practices, such as the use of metal coinage for trade. Before he left in 54 BC, Caesar made alliances with several of these tribes, including the Catuvellauni and the Atrebates. This gave access to the region to Roman traders, who soon imported Italian wine, pottery and fine silverware, in exchange for British produce (Webster 1980: 53). There is evidence of rapid agricultural development in the territory of the Trinovantes in this period, which may indicate that British chieftains attempted to increase the production of cereals to pay for Roman luxury goods (Webster 1980: 49).

When the Romans returned to Britain in force in AD 43, the south-east was the region most easily brought under Roman control. The emperor Claudius gave a large part of this area to a 'client king' called Cogidubnus, whom he made a Roman citizen. The king adopted the emperor's names, as recorded in an inscription from a temple to Jupiter and Minerva, found near Chichester, in which he is described as 'Tiberius Claudius Cogidubnus, great king of the Britons' (Webster 1981: 25). The 'hillfort' zone to the west proved much more resistant, however. Soon after the Roman invasion, the new governor Plautius sent the *legio II Augusta* under the command of the future emperor Vespasian into the lands of the hostile Durotriges, where he took a number of hillforts, including Maiden Castle and Hod Hill in southern England.

By the time Plautius left Britain in AD 47, the new province of Britannia extended to a line running from the mouth of the River Trent to the Severn estuary. Successive governors fought to conquer the territories of the tribes to the west and north of this frontier. The Silures and Ordovices resisted a Roman 'peace' until their territory was finally subjugated by Agricola, who began his long governorship in AD 77. After subduing the tribes of what is now Wales, Agricola headed north and attempted to extend Roman control across the whole of Britain. He won an overwhelming victory over a coalition of northern tribes in AD 83, and his fleet completed the first circumnavigation of the island. Soon after Agricola was recalled the following year, however, Roman troops were withdrawn and his gains in the far north were abandoned. A new frontier was established from the Solway Firth to the estuary of the River Tyne, which would later become the northerly limit of the Roman Empire and is known today as 'Hadrian's Wall'.

north of Britannia was created by an alliance with the Brigantes, a group of tribes ruled by their queen Cartimandua, who had formed a coalition with a yet more northerly tribe through her marriage to its leader Venutius. Claudius then returned to Rome, leaving Plautius to finish pacifying the conquered territory and create a stable frontier.

?Mons Graupius, AD 83

CALEDONII

Taus (Tay)

Taus (Firth of Tay)

Bodotria (Forth)

Bodotria (Firth of Forth)

Clota (Clyde)

Clota (Firth of Clyde)

NOVANTAE

Vindolanda

DUMNONII

BRIGANTES

PARISI

Humber estuary

Invasion of Mona, AD 60

Mona (Anglesey)

DECEANGLI

Deva (Chester)

CORTIELTAVI

Trisantona (Trent)

ICENI

?Caratacus' last battle, AD 50

ORDOVICES

Sabrina (Severn)

DOBUNNI

CATUVELLAUNI

TRINOVANTES

SILURES

Glevum (Gloucester)

Camulodunum (Colchester)

ATREBATES

Tamesis (Thames)

CANTIACI

Rutupiae (Richborough)

REGNI

Medway

BELGAE

DUROTRIGES

DUMNONII

N

0   50 miles

0   50km

The Opposing Sides

RECRUITMENT AND TRAINING

Roman

The Roman Army of the 1st century AD reflected the social divisions inherent in the empire as a whole: between slave and free-born, Roman citizen and provincial subject, aristocrat and commoner. Slaves were not permitted to join the Army. Nor were freedmen (those born into slavery but granted freedom later in life), though when the empire was desperately short of soldiers, special units were raised from freedmen and slaves manumitted for the purpose. The legions, the specialist heavy infantry that formed the core of the Roman Army, were only open to freeborn Roman citizens, most of whom lived in the Italian peninsula and southern Gaul. The auxiliary cavalry and infantry (from the Latin word *auxilia* – literally 'the help') were recruited from the vast population of the many provinces of the empire. These *peregrini* lived under imperial rule but did not enjoy the same status as citizens. Senior officers of both the legions and the auxiliary units were drawn from the ruling equestrian and senatorial classes, who were eligible to hold political office. Military service for them was essential in order to progress through the ranks of the imperial hierarchy.

Service in the legions was voluntary. Legionaries usually joined as young men of 17 or older, and remained in the Army for 25 years, should they live that long. They were reasonably well paid, at least in relation to free agricultural labourers, and could expect regular meals, a high standard of accommodation when not on campaign, and the prospect of rewards and their share of any spoils or bounty gained in war. At least some of the cost of food and lodging was deducted from soldiers' pay, however, and they had to purchase their own equipment, which would have been an expensive initial outlay. Legionaries were not allowed to marry, though informal relationships were common.

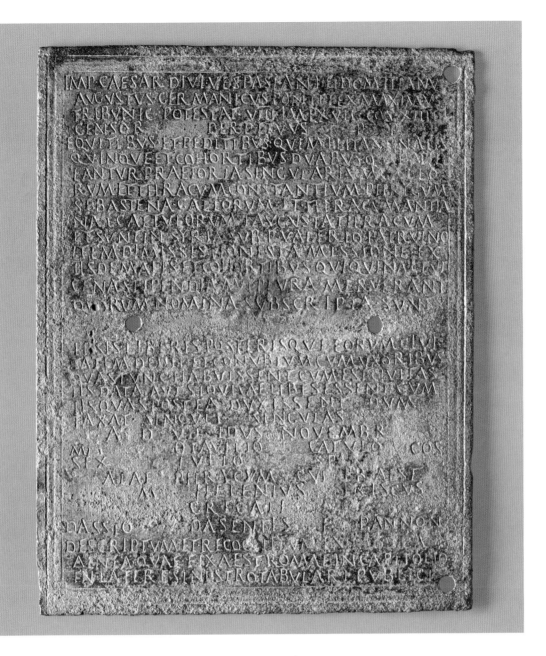

Legionary service was hard and dangerous. In the 1st century AD, legionaries could expect to spend their entire career on campaign or in a garrison far from home, and they constantly faced the prospect of being wounded or killed in battle. Legionaries were often tasked with major construction projects, such as building forts and roads, which involved tough physical labour. They were also subject to strict rules and harsh discipline: punishment could include beatings and even death for serious crimes. The legions would have drawn the majority of their recruits from poorer, mostly unskilled urban citizens, for whom an arduous military life was an attractive alternative to one of irregular employment and potential poverty.

One plaque of a diploma dating from AD 88, granting citizenship to a Roman auxiliary soldier and his descendants, issued during the reign of the emperor Domitian. Military diplomas like this often became treasured family possessions and were handed down through several generations. (Sepia Times/UIG via Getty Images)

Roman auxiliary soldier

The Roman auxiliary infantryman is about 25 years old. He has been in Britain for seven years, since he was recruited in his Batavian homeland in the Rhine delta and sent as a reinforcement to *cohors IX Batavorum*. He has participated in all of Agricola's campaigns in northern Britain. He has been fighting for several minutes so he is hot under his helmet and armour, and he is sweating and wet from the drizzly rain that has been falling all morning. His feet and lower legs are covered in thin, black mud from walking across peat bogs on the moorland, and his face, right hand and arm are spattered with blood. He is in the front rank of his century, which has engaged a band of Caledonian warriors. He has just punched an enemy warrior in the face with the boss of his shield and is about to stab him in the stomach with his short sword.

Weapons, dress and equipment

This infantry soldier has already thrown his two *hastae*, and is now fighting with his short, sharply pointed sword (*gladius*; **1**), designed for stabbing rather than cutting; and his flat, oval shield (*scutum*; **2**), which has a metal boss (*umbo*) in the centre, covering a horizontal handgrip. He uses the shield as a weapon as much as a means of defence: he can punch his enemy in the face with the metal boss, or shove him aside with his shoulder against the board. The back of the boss is filled with wool and horsehair to protect his knuckles. If he loses or breaks his sword, he will use his wide-bladed dagger (*pugio*; **3**) as a back-up weapon.

His copper-alloy helmet (*galea*; **4**) has an extension at the back to cover his neck and a reinforcement on the brow to deflect downward sword cuts. Hinged cheek pieces, with scallops around the eyes and mouth, protect his face. His ears are also uncovered so he can still see,

hear and communicate with those around him. Over a thick, woollen tunic (*tunica*; **5**) he wears a *lorica hamata* (**6**), which is made from small, interlocking iron rings. At around 9kg, it is heavy but very flexible and covers his torso, abdomen and groin, and gives excellent protection against cuts and thrusts from any angle. In the cold and wet of northern Britain he is grateful for his woollen breeches (*braccae*; **7**), and his closed leather boots (*caligae*; **8**), which have iron studs nailed into the soles to give some much-needed grip on the muddy ground.

Roman soldiers were fond of personal ornament. This auxiliary infantryman is no exception: his sword and dagger scabbards are beautifully, though cheaply, decorated; his crossed belts (*baltei*; **9**) are covered in embossed plates, which have been coated in tin to give them a 'silver' appearance; and he sports an impressive 'apron' of studded leather straps (**10**) that jingles when he moves.

The conquered territories that made up the provinces of the Roman Empire paid taxes in the form of money, raw materials and agricultural commodities, and they also had to provide their share of men for the auxiliary units of the Roman Army. These auxiliary units were made up of a mixture of volunteers and conscripts. Auxiliaries could look forward to a similar life to their legionary counterparts, albeit with lower pay. From the reign of the emperor Claudius, however, after 25 years' service auxiliary soldiers could be granted citizenship for themselves and for their children. This was a significant incentive and must have been an important attraction that greatly increased the number of volunteers.

The provision of young men for the Roman Army could be a burden on provincial communities, particularly those with a predominantly rural population. The Batavi, a tribal group who lived in a small area of the Rhine delta, had a special treaty relationship with the Roman Empire, and were exempt from all taxes except for the supply of men to serve in the Army. This was partly in recognition of Batavian loyalty in earlier campaigns in the region but also because the Romans believed the Batavi made particularly good soldiers, renowned for their ability to swim in full armour, and cross rivers that were impassable to other troops. In his comprehensive study of the Roman auxiliaries, the historian Ian Haynes describes (2013: 112–16) the enormous contribution made by the Batavians to the Roman Army: in the 1st century AD the Batavi provided eight cohorts (auxiliary units of infantry or mixed infantry and mounted soldiers) and one *ala*, as well as imperial bodyguards and sailors. This may have been as many as 5,500 men at any one time, from a total community of perhaps only 30,000–40,000 people.

On top of the chance of citizenship, for the young men of the Batavi the Roman Army held additional attractions. Warfare was a major part of Batavian life, and martial skills and arms and armour were highly valued; burials of Batavian men contained weapons long after the practice was abandoned elsewhere. The equipment of an auxiliary infantryman or cavalryman in the Roman Army – a metal helmet; armour made from iron 'mail' or scales; a sword, shield and spear – was that usually associated with an elite warrior or chief; enlisting in the Roman Army would have given Batavian youths enhanced status immediately. Even accepting these attractions, however, such a large contribution of manpower from a small community could not have been achieved without conscription. To begin with, the Batavian nobility provided entire irregular units to the Roman Army, which they led themselves. Ties of kinship and obligation would have made calling up sufficient numbers of men relatively easy, and the soldiers' loyalty would have been to their own leaders. In AD 69, during the civil wars that followed the death of the emperor Nero (r. AD 54–68), the Batavi revolted against their treaty obligations, partly because Roman officers attempted to levy the Batavians directly, rather than through the Batavian nobility. After the revolt, the Batavian auxiliary units were regularized, though they appear to have been still led by their own nobles, albeit serving as Roman officers.

Although it would be 25 years until an auxiliary recruit was granted citizenship, his incorporation into the Roman Empire began the day he joined up; a soldier's career began with the swearing of an oath of allegiance to the emperor, in Latin. Auxiliary recruits would have had to learn Latin quickly (citizens joining the legions would have been more likely to be fluent already) in order to receive orders and communicate with their superiors and the other soldiers in their unit. Auxiliary soldiers often adopted Roman names upon enlistment, to help them fit in, and because their original names may have been difficult for officers to pronounce (Haynes 2013: 101 & 302). Although he might never learn to read or write Latin or Greek, we can assume that a soldier would have been able to recognize his own (adopted) name because so many weapons and pieces of military equipment have been found that are inscribed with the owner's name, and the name of his unit.

The training of Roman soldiers was described by the writer Vegetius (4th century AD) in his treatise on the Roman Army, *Epitome of Military Science* (1.8–28). Although Vegetius wrote at least three centuries after the Roman invasion of Britain, he is considered to have based much of his work on that of earlier authors who described the Roman Army in the 1st century AD. Recruit training began with physical exercises. Recruits learnt how to march at a quick pace, in step with their comrades over long distances and carrying a heavy burden of personal equipment and supplies; how to run in full armour and cross obstacles; and how to swim. If they could not do so already, recruits were taught to ride, and they practised vaulting onto a horse's back from both the right and left side. They then trained to fight in the Roman manner with a short, stabbing sword, known as a *gladius*, and a large wooden shield called a *scutum*. Soldiers practised with special wooden swords and wicker shields that weighed twice as much as the real thing in order to build up their strength and stamina and develop an efficient fighting technique. Roman soldiers needed to learn not to waste energy with unnecessary movements so they did not become exhausted too quickly on the battlefield. Recruits also learnt to cast javelins, how to use a sling and how to shoot a bow and arrow. Later, recruits were drilled in battlefield manoeuvres such as establishing a 'wedge' formation before an attack and how to create a *testudo* ('tortoise') formation, interlocking their shields into a wall and roof to protect themselves from enemy missiles. They were also taught how to dig trenches and build camps and fortifications.

British Celt

We know much less about the society of the Celts, particularly in Britain, and the scant information we do have refers to Celtic peoples across Europe, and over several hundred years. It would be foolish to believe that what applied in one region and time was necessarily the case for another, but it is possible to make some general observations. Celtic society was as divided as that of the Roman Empire, with one exception: for the Celts there was no distinction between 'soldier' and 'civilian'. All free males would learn to handle weapons and fight when necessary, which was often: warfare was an essential element of Celtic life. Neighbouring and rival groups were in a constant state of low-level conflict as tribes fluctuated between alliance and feud.

Julius Caesar wrote a vivid account of his campaigns and ultimate subjugation of Gaul. His *Gallic Wars* contains much detail about the Celts, or 'Gauls' as the Romans called them. According to Caesar, Celtic society

A Roman *denarius* depicting a naked Celtic warrior carrying a shield riding in a chariot pulled by two ponies. A *carnyx* is shown in the background. The British Celts were among the last peoples in Europe to employ the chariot in warfare. (Werner Forman/Universal Images Group/Getty Images)

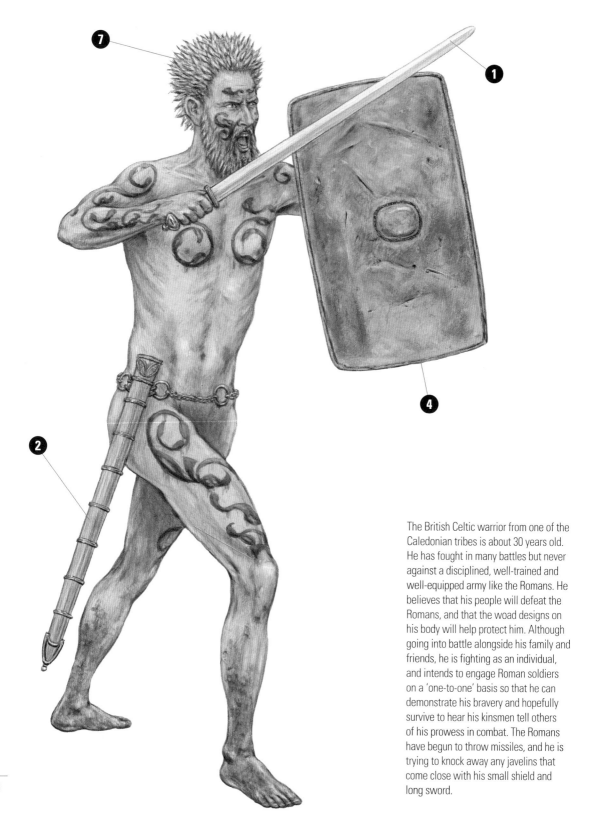

The British Celtic warrior from one of the Caledonian tribes is about 30 years old. He has fought in many battles but never against a disciplined, well-trained and well-equipped army like the Romans. He believes that his people will defeat the Romans, and that the woad designs on his body will help protect him. Although going into battle alongside his family and friends, he is fighting as an individual, and intends to engage Roman soldiers on a 'one-to-one' basis so that he can demonstrate his bravery and hopefully survive to hear his kinsmen tell others of his prowess in combat. The Romans have begun to throw missiles, and he is trying to knock away any javelins that come close with his small shield and long sword.

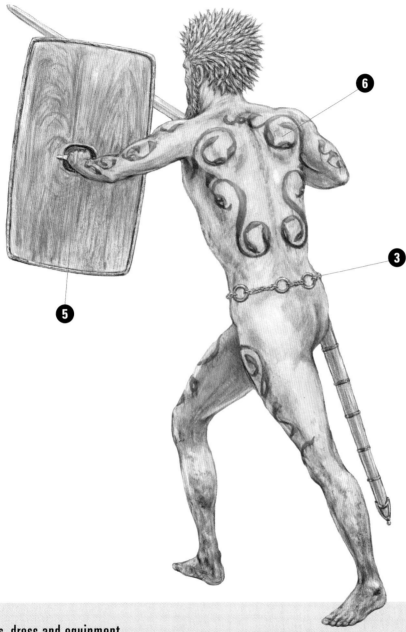

Weapons, dress and equipment

This British warrior has drawn his iron sword (**1**), which has a long blade about 70cm long and a rounded tip. It is designed for slashing and cutting, and the warrior needs plenty of space to wield it effectively in battle. The sword scabbard (**2**) is made of ash wood and is decorated with ornately worked copper-alloy fittings. It is a valuable weapon that the warrior inherited from his father, and he wears it proudly. The sword scabbard is suspended on his right hip from a copper-alloy chain (**3**) in such a way that it hangs straight down and does not interfere with his leg as he moves. In his left hand the warrior holds up his small, leather-covered wooden shield (**4**), which has a recess cut into it for a horizontal handgrip (**5**). The shield is light and easy to manoeuvre, but the warrior will find that it provides scant protection against sharp-pointed Roman swords and javelins.

Without armour or a helmet, or even clothes, the warrior relies on the magical properties of his blue body-paint (**6**) to protect him from injury. The paint is made from woad and the designs are inspired by Celtic religious symbols and animals and birds. He hopes his appearance will also intimidate his Roman enemies. He has bleached his hair (**7**) with lime, and dressed it into spikes with animal fat to make himself look even more frightening.

Obverse of a coin issued by Cunobeline, king of the British Catuvellauni tribe *c*.AD 10–40. It carries an image of a shield and the face of some kind of animal or mythical creature, and the word 'CAMU', the first four letters of the name of Cunobeline's capital, Camulodumum. (Heritage Arts/Heritage Images via Getty Images)

Two galloping horses and a wheel are depicted on the reverse of the Cunobeline coin, presumably signifying a chariot. (Sepia Times/Universal Images Group via Getty Images)

was dominated by two groups: religious leaders known as the 'druids', and a nobility, or 'warrior elite', who led their tribes in peace and war (*Gallic Wars* 6.15). The warrior elite defined themselves and their households through success in battle. Their heroism was recorded orally and recounted by retainers to impress guests at feasts and to intimidate enemies before two sides clashed. The warrior elites' power depended on the number of retainers and clients upon whom they could call to support them when they decided to go to war. Warriors themselves could also be clients of other more powerful warlords, so that when one tribal group moved against another, subservient warriors would be expected to bring their fighters in support (Cunliffe 1997: 108). Other warriors were joined by mutual bonds of friendship, which could be very powerful. Caesar described an attack by a Celtic commander called Adiatunnus, who led a force of 600 men known as *soldurii*, who were so committed to one another that if they were not killed in battle at the same time, they would even commit suicide upon the death of their friends (*Gallic Wars* 3.22). The Greek historian Polybius recorded (*Histories* 2.22–31) how a similar warrior group called the *Gaesatae* (literally 'spearmen') joined a massed Celtic attack on northern Italy in 225 BC. The *Gaesatae* were a group of mercenaries who would fight for any other tribe who would pay them. At the battle of Telamon in 225 BC, they faced the Romans naked apart from their weapons, and fought bravely in the front ranks of the Celtic army. Through such ties of patronage and friendship, the Celts could quickly muster large armies, like those that fought the Roman Army during the Roman conquest of Britain.

Celtic warriors would have learnt to use weapons from an early age. Boys would have started with a spear, which could have been thrust or thrown, as well as the more specialized javelin, because they were essential hunting tools. Another hunting weapon, the sling, was also mastered early. As the Biblical David proved, though too young to fight hand to hand, boys could still be deadly with a sling, particularly in defence of a fortification; large stores of slingstones have been found buried behind the gateways of hillforts in southern Britain. As they reached manhood, Celtic warriors would have trained in the use of sword and shield. Celtic swords were long, slashing weapons, with iron blades that could be up to 90cm from hilt guard to tip, and were most effective when wielded overhead to slice at an enemy's head, shoulders and arms. This technique required a great deal of strength but also stamina, as it would have been very tiring to repeatedly swing such a long sword during battle. Shields were also large and heavy, and Celtic warriors used them to fend off enemy sword blows and spear thrusts, but also as protection from missiles such as slingstones and arrows. Young Celtic warriors must have spent much of their time training with these weapons to develop the strength and fitness needed to become proficient. Fighting was so common among Celtic tribes that they would not have had to wait long before they would have the opportunity to hone these skills in combat.

The Celts were excellent horsemen. Celtic cavalry was used to great effect in Hannibal's Carthaginian army, and much of the auxiliary cavalry of the Roman Army was supplied by Celtic communities from Gaul. The Celtic cavalry would have been formed by the warrior elites and their senior retainers,

who would have learnt to ride and fight from the saddle in childhood. The Celts did not have stirrups but developed a saddle made from wood and leather that had 'horns' at each corner, which gripped the horseman's thighs and held him so securely that he could throw javelins, and fight with spear, sword and shield. This design of saddle was so effective that it also became standard equipment for Roman cavalry.

The British Celts were the last people in Europe to employ the chariot in battle. When Julius Caesar first invaded Britain in 55 BC, he was so taken back by the British use of the chariot that he included a long account of it in his *Gallic Wars* (4.33). Each chariot normally carried a crew of two: an elite warrior and a driver, or charioteer. At the beginning of a battle, the charioteer would drive his vehicle in all directions in front of the enemy, while the warrior threw javelins, causing confusion and panic, before the warrior dismounted and fought on foot. The charioteer then withdrew to a safe distance, but remained ready to return and retrieve the warrior from danger

Dating from *c.*300 BC, this Celtic helmet with a complex crest in the shape of a bird was found in a grave in Ciumeşti in Romania and is now in the Muzeul National de Istorie, Bucharest. The wings are hinged and would have flapped when the warrior moved. Helmets with animal-shaped crests are described by the Greek historian Diodorus Siculus (*Library of History* 5.30), and shown on one of the panels of the 'Gundestrup Cauldron'. (DEA/G. DAGLI ORTI/De Agostini via Getty Images)

or swiftly carry him to another part of the battlefield. As Caesar remarked, in this way the chariot provided the British Celts with the manoeuvrability of cavalry and the resilience of infantry. British charioteers were extraordinarily skilful: through constant practice they learnt to control their chariots at full speed on any terrain and the steepest of slopes. When necessary, they could run forward along the beam connecting the chariot to the horses, and leap back again like gymnasts.

ORGANIZATION AND LEADERSHIP

Roman

The organization of the Roman Army in the 1st century AD was clearly explained by the historian Brian Dobson, and artist and historian Peter Connolly (2016: 216–28). The core was formed by the 30 legions. Even on its own, a legion was a powerful force, with an ideal strength of around 5,500 heavily armed and armoured infantry citizen-soldiers. A legion was divided into ten smaller tactical units, called cohorts, which in turn were divided into centuries. The first cohort was nearly twice the size of the other nine, with five centuries of around 160 men each. The other cohorts were made up of six centuries of about 80 men each. Each legion was accompanied by a small cavalry unit of 120 mounted troopers, who would carry out essential dispatch riding and scouting duties (Connolly 2016: 216).

The auxiliary infantry was also organized into cohorts, initially with an ideal strength of 500 soldiers, divided into six centuries. Later in the 1st century AD, larger cohorts were formed, with ten centuries and a strength of around 1,000 men (although in practice this was probably only 800, as each century contained 80 men). The auxiliary cavalry was organized into *alae* (literally 'wings', from their traditional position on the 'wings' of a Roman army on the battlefield). Like the auxiliary cohorts, the *alae* could have a strength of either 500 or 1,000 men, divided into *turmae*. The *turma* was the cavalry equivalent of the infantry century, and was made up of about 32 cavalry troopers. A further type of mixed auxiliary unit, known as the *cohors equitata*, combined 6–10 infantry centuries and 4–8 mounted *turmae* (Connolly 2016: 223–24).

The smallest unit in both the legions and the auxiliary infantry formations was the century, which was normally composed of 80 men. The infantry century, whether legionary or auxiliary, was commanded by a centurion. His equivalent in the cavalry was a decurion, who commanded a *turma* (squadron) of 32 mounted troopers. According to Connolly (2016: 220–21), in the legions, the centurion was normally promoted from the ranks and was a soldier of experience, ability and bravery. Their casualty rate was high: a centurion led his century into battle from the front, and would be expected to hold his position to the very end if necessary. Centurions' armour and equipment were distinctive: they wore a 'transverse' crest on their helmet so they could be recognized in a throng, and often wore armour that had been coated with tin to give it a 'silver' appearance. Centurions wore their sword on the left hip and their dagger on the right hip – the opposite way around

to the ordinary legionary – and often also wore lower leg armour, or greaves. In camp, a centurion carried a *vitis*, his traditional symbol of office, which was a stout stick cut from the stem of a grapevine. The centurion used his *vitis* to discipline the soldiers of his century, sometimes severely. Each century and *turma* was known by the name of its commander. Hence, we find weapons and equipment inscribed with the name of the owner and the name of the centurion or decurion who commanded the owner's unit. The most senior centurions in a legion commanded the double-strength centuries of the first cohort, and the highest ranking of all was the *primus pilus*, literally 'first spear'.

The Roman Army was not just a formidable fighting force; it was also a complex bureaucracy, which relied on the written word. Therefore, in order to perform their duties, both centurions and decurions needed to be able to read and write Latin, and in the eastern provinces of the Roman Empire, also Greek. Every day, centurions would submit written reports on the status of their unit to their commanding officers, and also had to write requests for food and equipment, intelligence reports, leave passes for their men, inventories and a host of other documents. Among auxiliary soldiers, fluency in Latin was much less prevalent than among the citizen legionaries. To ensure that units were commanded by men with the requisite administrative skills, it was sometimes necessary for auxiliary centurions and decurions to be appointed directly (Haynes 2013: 326). These may have been experienced centurions drafted in from the legions or, in the case of units raised from allied peoples

Relief panel from the gravestone of Titus Calidius Severus, *c.*1st century AD, showing the armour of a centurion: helmet with a transverse crest, 'scale' armour and greaves. Titus Calidius Severus had a long and interesting military career. He enlisted as a mounted trooper in a mixed infantry and cavalry unit, the *cohors I Alpinorum equitata*, rising to the rank of decurion in command of a *turma* of 32 horsemen. He then became a centurion in the *legio XV Apollinaris.* (DEA/A. DAGLI ORTI/De Agostini via Getty Images)

such as the Batavi, educated men from wealthier families whose leadership status among their own people was recognized on enlistment.

The more senior officers of the legions and *auxilia* were normally temporary appointees. Military service was part of the political career structure of the Roman elite. A legion was commanded by a legionary legate, who was a member of the Roman senate appointed by the emperor. A legate was normally a junior senator who would command a legion before becoming a governor of an entire province. He was assisted by six tribunes. The other senior officer in a legion was the camp prefect, who was often a former *primus pilus* and was responsible for equipment and logistics. He was effectively third-in-command of a legion after the legate and most senior tribune. The auxiliary cohorts were commanded by a prefect, who was a young man of the elite equestrian order appointed by the provincial governor, rather than the emperor. Able prefects might progress to the command of a 1,000-strong cohort or the rank of junior tribune in a legion, before ultimately taking command of a cavalry *ala* (Connolly 2016: 224).

Some auxiliary units were commanded by members of the provincial elite from the area in which the unit was originally raised. According to the Roman historian Tacitus, prior to their revolt during the civil war of AD 69, the Batavi had fought in Britain, where they were commanded by their own nobles (*Histories* 4.12). In the late AD 90s, the *cohors IX Batavorum* formed

 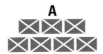

part of the garrison of the fort at Vindolanda, near modern-day Hexham in Northumberland, where excavations have revealed deposits of organic objects that have been preserved in the unique anaerobic conditions of the wet, acidic soil. Among the objects discovered are a large number of wooden writing tablets, on which letters, reports and other documents have been written in ink. It is clear from the contents of these 'Vindolanda tablets' that the prefect of the *cohors IX Batavorum* at that time was Flavius Cerialis. One of the tablets (Tab. Vindol. III.628) is a letter to Flavius Cerialis from a decurion named Masculus, asking for instructions about where his unit was to travel the next day. In his greeting Masculus addresses Cerialis as 'my king'. It has been suggested by the historian David Cuff (2011: 146) that this is a recognition of Flavius Cerialis' joint status as a descendant of the Batavian nobility and officer in the Roman Army. Interestingly, as a postscript, Masculus asks his commander for more beer, as his men have run out.

British Celt

Julius Caesar wrote that power in Celtic society was concentrated in the hands of two classes of men. The warrior elite, or 'knights' as Caesar called them, were the Celts' political and military leaders, and the druids governed spiritual and religious matters. In Caesar's analysis, the rest of the population were little more than slaves, completely dependent on the patronage and support of the elite warrior they served (*Gallic Wars* 6.13). As the eminent archaeologist Barry Cunliffe has observed (1997: 107), however, Caesar grossly simplified what must have been a complex hierarchical society. Between the most powerful nobles, who had thousands of retainers, and the poorest dependent farmers, there would have been a spectrum of recognizable social classes. Unfortunately, we know little about them. Just as in Roman society, class distinctions would have been enforced by law but also through social conventions such as the way a person dressed, the jewellery they wore or the weapons carried by a warrior. Even hairstyles could have signified a person's status. According to the Greek historian Diodorus Siculus, the Celts cut their facial hair in different ways. Some men were clean-shaven, others had short beards, while the nobles shaved only their cheeks and let their moustaches grow so long that they covered their mouths (*Library of History* 5.28). The British Celtic practice of decorating

There are few detailed descriptions in the literary works of ancient authors of the formation of the Roman Army on the battlefield in the 1st century AD. This diagram shows a theoretical Roman battle line formed by an army of two legions and associated auxiliary units, based on the available evidence (Pollard & Berry 2015: 46). According to Tacitus (*Annals* 14.34), when Paulinus confronted Boudicca's army in AD 60, the legions formed the centre of the battle line (**A**), with auxiliary infantry on each flank (**B**), and the auxiliary cavalry arranged in wings on the far right and left (**C**). The infantry usually formed up in two or three lines, depending on the terrain and the relative strength of the enemy. The cavalry *alae* would probably have been reinforced with the mounted *turmae* from mixed cohorts. In most battles, the Roman commander would keep a number of infantry (**D**) and cavalry (**E**) units in reserve, to be deployed where the course of the battle demanded. A small cavalry unit (not shown here) may have accompanied each legion.

the body with blue woad, as observed by Caesar when he first arrived on the island (*Gallic Wars* 5.14), may also have had a role in the communication of social status.

Celtic warriors achieved power and increased the size of their retinues by winning in battle. Warfare was an essential part of Celtic life, providing constant opportunity for a warrior to demonstrate his bravery and fighting skills. As the historian James Fraser has pointed out, only the most senior centurions in the Roman Army would have gained as much experience of combat and leadership on the battlefield as a powerful Celtic chieftain (Fraser 2008: 42). This experience could be both gained and demonstrated in single combat. According to Diodorus Siculus (*Library of History* 5.29), when two Celtic armies drew near for battle, it was common for elite warriors to step forward of their own lines and challenge any one of his enemy who felt brave enough to fight him alone. If this challenge was accepted, the warrior would regale his opponent with stories of the brave deeds of his ancestors and his own great achievements. Single combat was more than just a way for a warrior to build a reputation as a great fighter. It also limited the potential for members of opposing tribes to be killed or wounded. If a conflict could be resolved with the defeat or victory of only one or several warriors, both sides could return to their settlements almost intact (Cunliffe 1997: 102).

Dating from the 1st century AD and normally identified as a statue of a Celtic warrior, this could be a portrait of an auxiliary cavalryman. Note the detail of the shoulder reinforcement on the mail armour and the buckle on the shield belt. The warrior wears a torc around his neck. (DEA/A. DAGLI ORTI/De Agostini via Getty Images)

Among the British Celts, women could hold political and military power. Tacitus noted that the British Celts made no distinction between men and women when they chose their leaders (*Agricola* 16). Boudicca, who famously led the Iceni in a violent rebellion against Roman rule in AD 60, took control of her tribe when her husband Prasutagus, king of the Iceni, died. Another powerful female leader was Cartimandua, who ruled the large confederation of tribes known as the Brigantes, whose territory stretched across much of what is now Yorkshire and Lancashire in northern England. Cartimandua was a staunch Roman ally, upon whom successive governors relied to keep more northerly hostile tribes out of the province of Britannia.

The so-called 'Witham Shield', named after the river in Lincolnshire in which it was found, is now on display in the British Museum in London. Dating from the 4th century BC, this beautifully manufactured copper-alloy object is actually only the decorative cover for a shield, and would originally have been fixed to a wooden board. The image of a boar is inscribed on the surface. It is unlikely that such a fine piece would have been used in battle. It was probably intended for parade or ritual purposes, or may have been made specifically to be deposited in the river as an offering. (Werner Forman/Universal Images Group/Getty Images)

A

C

B

This diagram shows how a theoretical British Celtic army may have formed up for battle, based on the available evidence. The British Celts still used chariots in battle (**A**), which would range across the battlefield in front of the infantry, often accompanied by cavalry. When Boudicca massed her enormous rebel force against Paulinus' Roman army in AD 60, Tacitus (*Annals* 14.34) describes the British as ranging over a wide area, in 'bands' of infantry (**B**) and cavalry (**C**), in stark contrast to the disciplined Roman formations.

The practice of selecting women as leaders of Celtic tribes may have been unique to Britain (Cunliffe 1997: 110).

We know very little about how the British Celts organized themselves on the battlefield. There clearly was a unit structure of some kind, albeit a much less formal one than found in the Roman Army. The Celts carried standards into battle, just like the Romans, which would have identified particular groups and acted as rallying points on the battlefield. Examples of these standards, which often took the form of flags, or statues of animals and birds, can be seen in the portrayal of captured Celtic weapons and equipment on monuments such as the Triumphal Arch of Orange in south-west France. The Celts' *carnyces* may also have been used to send signals during battle, as well as frighten and intimidate an enemy (Connolly 2016: 114–15). Celtic 'units' would have been formed by the retainers and kinsmen of powerful elite warriors or chieftains, and would have varied greatly in strength.

RELIGION AND BELIEFS

Roman

The observance of religious ritual governed all aspects of Roman public and private life. The Romans worshipped an enormous variety of gods and goddesses, from the most important 'Gods of the Capitol' in Rome itself – Jupiter, Juno and Minerva – to local provincial deities and household spirits. The Romans even worshipped the emperors, living and dead, and members of their family. As the empire grew, and contact increased with cultures beyond the frontiers, the worship of foreign deities also spread across Roman territory, creating a hugely diverse spiritual universe in which Roman soldiers, both citizen legionary and subject auxiliary, were fully immersed.

Our understanding of Roman military religion comes from a number of sources. The works of Roman writers describe some of the ceremonies that Roman soldiers attended, and there are many surviving inscriptions on altars dedicated to different gods by serving and retired Roman soldiers. A fascinating papyrus document known as the *feriale Duranum* was recovered from the remains of a large Roman fortress built at the city of Dura-Europos (in modern-day eastern Syria). Archaeologists have found an enormous collection of armour, weapons, equipment and papyrus documents buried at Dura-Europos, which was abandoned after it was lost to the Sassanid Empire

in AD 256–57. Unusually, no later settlement was built upon the ruins and the very dry conditions preserved a huge amount of material, which would otherwise have perished. The *feriale Duranum* is the calendar of an auxiliary cohort, the *cohors XX Palmyrenorum*, and it lists all the most important festivals celebrated by that unit. Historians believe that it is likely that these festivals were marked by units across the Roman Army because there is no mention of any rituals specific to the *cohors XX Palmyrenorum*, or any local deities (Goldsworthy 2011: 90 & 108). As well as festivals held to worship the most important Roman gods, ceremonies mentioned in the *feriale Duranum* included those associated with *honestio missio*, in which soldiers whose service was complete received their honourable discharge from the Roman Army (Haynes 2013: 200).

The *feriale Duranum* also included many festivals celebrating the birthdays and other important dates in the lives of the emperors. 'Emperor worship' was particularly important for the Roman Army because soldiers ultimately owed their loyalty to the emperor alone. Roman soldiers swore an oath of allegiance to the emperor upon enlistment, known as the *sacramentum*, and it was renewed every year. It was so important that some soldiers even

Plaster cast of a scene from Trajan's Column, AD 113, showing Roman legionaries in *lorica segmentata* body armour and carrying curved, rectangular shields. (Leemage/Universal Images Group via Getty Images)

venerated a spirit, or *genius*, associated with the oath itself (Haynes 2013: 216; Goldsworthy 2011: 109). In a fort or barracks the emperor's image was everywhere, in the form of statues, busts and portraits, alongside images of gods and goddesses. The emperor's face also decorated every coin in a soldier's purse, and in the first part of the 1st century AD, images of the imperial family were common on soldiers' equipment such as sword scabbards and dagger sheaths (Haynes 2013: 213–16). The complete incorporation of the worship of the emperors into wider religious celebration constantly reminded Roman soldiers of the reason for their loyalty: the empire they served was so favoured by the gods that its emperors were divine themselves.

Roman soldiers held particular reverence for their standards. Roman Army standards were the insignia of each unit. The main standard of a legion was the *aquila* or eagle, and was made from gold. A legion also carried an *imago*, a carving of the face of the emperor; a *vexillum*, which was a special flag; and a symbol or totem unique to each legion, often in the form of an animal or sign of the zodiac. Every individual century also carried its own standard, called a *signum*. Soldiers would celebrate important dates in the history of their unit in ceremonies involving their standards, and every year the Roman Army held festivals known as the *Rosaliae signorum*, for which the standards were decorated with garlands of roses.

The private religious observance of Roman soldiers was just as varied. As long as they were seen to fully embrace their public and military religious obligations, Roman soldiers appear to have enjoyed a great amount of private religious freedom. Soldiers are known to have venerated many deities that originated in the provinces of the Roman Empire, and which were spread across Roman territory by the movement of Roman Army units. Batavian and Tungrian auxiliaries, who were recruited into the Roman Army from the lower-Rhine, are particularly associated with the worship of a god called Hercules Magusanus. It appears that Magusanus was a god local to the lower-Rhine, and when large numbers of tribesmen from this region joined the Roman Army in the first part of the 1st century AD, the similarity of their god with the Romano-Greek god Hercules led to the two gods being associated in the minds of worshippers. Dedications made by soldiers to Hercules Magusanus have been found as far apart as Edinburgh in Scotland and Gherla in Romania, as well as at Empel in Holland where the cult of Magusanus originated (Haynes 2013: 232–35).

British Celt

Julius Caesar included a concise account of the religion of the Gallic Celts in his *Gallic Wars* (6.13–20). He stated that the Celts were a very religious people, devoted to superstitious practices, who worshipped a number of male and female deities. In an effort to explain Celtic religion to his Roman audience, Caesar simplified the Celtic pantheon and equated some of their deities with the Roman gods Mercury, Jupiter, Mars, Minerva and Dis Pater, the Roman god of the dead, from whom Caesar said all Celts claimed descent (Cunliffe 1997: 185–87). The Roman poet Lucan described three Celtic gods, Teutates, Esus, and Taranis (*Pharsalia* 1. 441–51), and others are known from inscriptions and early Irish and Welsh literature (Cunliffe 1997: 185–87).

The Celts' relationship with their gods was mediated through the druids. The druids were a priestly caste who oversaw all religious ceremonies (including human sacrifice), arbitrated in disputes and passed judgement in criminal cases. According to Diodorus Siculus (*c*.90–30 BC), the druids even had the power to intervene to stop battles between opposing tribes (*Library of History* 5.31). Anyone who did not accept the decision of the druids was banned from sacrifices for life, and shunned by the rest of society. The druids were exempt from the obligation to fight in support of a tribal leader, and did not have to pay taxes.

The druids were highly educated, and spent many years in training. As well as learning how to conduct their religious rites, they were also taught about the nature of the universe, the movement of the stars and natural history. The druids committed all their teaching to memory, in order to keep it a secret from the rest of society, though they used the Greek alphabet

A Celtic *carnyx* with a 'bell' in the shape of a mythical serpent or dragon's head. This *carnyx* was one of seven discovered in a large hoard at Tintignac, central France, in 2004. Similar *carnyces* are portrayed in sculpture such as the Triumphal Arch of Orange, on coins, and on the silver 'Gundestrup Cauldron'. The Greek historian Polybius described (*Histories* 2.29) the intimidating sound of these Celtic war horns at the battle of Telamon in 225 BC; and another Greek author, Diodorus Siculus, felt that their 'harsh' sound suited the chaos of battle (*Library of History* 5.30). A recent project to recreate this instrument, and another example from Scotland known as the 'Deskford carnyx', has demonstrated that they were actually capable of producing a wide range of sounds, and when played softly, their subtle, intimate music was also fitting for use in ritual. (FRANÇOIS GUILLOT/AFP via Getty Images)

for day-to-day written communication and accounting (Caesar, *Gallic Wars* 6.14). Caesar understood that druidism began in Britain and spread from there to Gaul, and that when he was conquering Gaul in the middle of the 1st century BC, young druids would travel to Britain for further instruction (*Gallic Wars* 6.13).

The druids practised human sacrifice, in order to appease the power of the gods. The Greek geographer Strabo wrote that victims (who according to Caesar were usually criminals) were shot with arrows, impaled in temples or put into a huge statue made of straw and wood along with cattle and wild animals and burnt to death. Others were stabbed in the back by a druid, who would try to divine the future from their death struggles (*Geography* 4.4.5). The Romans professed abhorrence at these rituals, and used such practices as justification for a ruthless campaign to destroy the druids. In reality, however, druidic human sacrifice was not that different from a number of Roman practices, such as the sacrifice of slaves in ritual mortal combat at funerals, a grisly entertainment that developed into the bloody spectacle of the gladiatorial games. The Roman emperors wanted to stamp out druidism in their new provinces because it formed an unacceptable alternative power structure with influence over their subjects.

According to Cunliffe (1997: 209), at least until the beginning of the 1st century BC, bodies of the British Celts were not buried, as was common in continental Europe, but left in an exposed location to rot and be eaten by birds and animals – a practice known as excarnation. After the rest of the body had gone, the bones might have been collected by members of the deceased's family or tribe to be used in other rituals. The Celts believed that when they died their soul did not pass into the afterlife but was reborn into the body of another person. Caesar surmises that this might have explained why Celtic warriors were so brave in battle: they did not fear death because they

knew that only their present bodies would die and their souls would live on (*Gallic Wars* 6.14).

It was the Celts' belief that the soul resided in the head, which might explain the Celtic fondness for cutting off and keeping the heads of enemies killed in battle. Diodorus Siculus recounts (*Library of History* 5.29) how Celtic warriors would tie their gruesome trophies to their horses' necks, then nail them to the walls of their houses as some hunters do the horns of animals. Heads of powerful men would be embalmed in cedar oil to preserve them, and warriors would keep them in a special box so they could show them proudly to strangers. It seems the Celts believed that to possess a head was to possess and control the power of the dead person: the more heads a warrior owned, the more powerful the warrior (Cunliffe 1997: 210).

After a battle, the victors would collect all the armour and weapons of their defeated enemies and pile them up in sacred places (Caesar, *Gallic Wars* 6.17), or throw them into water, such as a lake, river or marsh as an offering to the gods of war. Much of the surviving Celtic militaria has been found deposited in such places. In Britain the Thames seems to have been a favoured site for weapon 'sacrifice': it was in this river that the famous horned 'Waterloo helmet' and the ornate 'Battersea shield' were discovered. Other precious objects such as clothing, food or horse equipment may also have been deposited, but because these items were made from organic materials, they have not survived.

The 'Gundestrup Cauldron' – an ornate silver vessel found in a bog in northern Denmark and the largest piece of Iron Age European silverwork yet discovered. Dated to *c.*150–1 BC and now in the Nationalmuseet in Copenhagen, it is decorated on the outside and inside with images of gods, animals and mythical beasts. The metalworking techniques and artistic style appear to be Thracian (from modern-day Romania or Bulgaria) but the animal-crested helmets and *carnyces* are Celtic. (DE AGOSTINI PICTURE LIBRARY/ Getty Images)

Caratacus' Last Stand

AD 50

BACKGROUND TO BATTLE

The new province of Britannia covered nearly all of southern and eastern Britain. As well as precious silver and iron-ore mines, this area contained the best agricultural land and was populated by those tribes who had been in contact with the Roman Empire and its culture for almost a century. Roman goods and the use of coinage in trade were widespread. Many of the tribes who lived across the frontier, however, in the more mountainous and wooded regions to the north and west, remained as hostile as the landscape was inhospitable.

Aulus Plautius, the commander of the Roman invasion force, was responsible for governing Britannia. He divided his legions and stationed them at strategic locations, and dispersed the auxiliary units on the frontiers. According to Webster (1981: 20), the *legio XX* was garrisoned at Cunobeline's old capital at Camulodunum; the *legio IX* on the edge of Iceni territory, near modern-day Peterborough; the *legio II* at Chichester on the south coast; and the *legio XIV* was likely to have been stationed at Leicester in the midlands.

Plautius left Britain in the winter of AD 47/48. He returned to Rome to great honour and a quiet retirement, leaving the province of Britannia relatively stable. Caratacus, however, remained a significant

Detail of the central boss of a copper-alloy shield cover found in the River Witham in Lincolnshire. (Universal History Archive/Universal Images Group via Getty Images)

threat. He had slipped across the River Severn into the territory of the Silures, who controlled much of what is now south Wales. He was gathering support for an attack on the Romans, and at the same time, using his network of contacts to foment rebellion within the province. Plautius' successor was Publius Ostorius Scapula, who waited in Gaul while Plautius left the island, to avoid both governors being in the province at the same time. For Caratacus, this was the perfect opportunity. It was winter and he hoped that the new governor would not expect an incursion, and that Scapula's lack of familiarity with the region and his own army would make him slow to react. Scapula landed in Britain to find his new province in chaos (Webster 1981: 14).

The events of Scapula's turbulent governorship, and his confrontation with Caratacus, are recorded by Tacitus in his *Annals of Imperial Rome* (12.31–39). Tacitus recounts that Scapula struck immediately at the hostile tribes with auxiliary units, presumably because he was not able to draw on legionary forces quickly enough. Scapula's swift action contained the uprising, but he was not able to capture Caratacus, who fell back to the lands of the Silures. To prevent further unrest within the province, Scapula resolved to disarm all the tribes south of the River Trent and the Severn. He must have sent soldiers into indigenous settlements, farms and homes to search for weapons. For the British tribesmen, and especially the warrior elite for whom warfare, and the ownership of arms, was an essential part of their daily lives, this must have been intolerable. As Webster has pointed out (1981: 21), few would have given up their swords and spears voluntarily; every household the Roman soldiers visited would have resisted, and many confrontations would have ended in violence. It is not surprising that this policy led to further unrest.

The first to revolt were the Iceni, supposedly Roman allies, who were joined by neighbouring tribes. Scapula advanced against them, again deploying an auxiliary force. The rebels assembled in a fortification surrounded by a rough earthen rampart, with a narrow entrance designed to make it impossible for cavalry to enter. Scapula commanded his cavalry to dismount and fight as infantry, and assaulted the fortification. The Roman forces quickly overcame the British warriors, who were trapped inside their own ramparts. News of the defeat of the Iceni soon dampened the spirit of rebellion in the rest of the province.

Dating from AD 107–08, this relief panel from the Tropaeum Traiani at Adamclisi in Romania was set up to commemorate the Roman soldiers who died in the Dacian campaigns of the emperor Trajan (r. AD 98–117). The soldiers wear cloaks and carry heavy javelins (*pila*) and curved, rectangular shields (*scuta*). Note that they wear their swords on the left hip. Legionaries would have normally worn their swords on the right hip. It is possible that the panel is supposed to represent a pair of centurions, who did wear their swords on the left, or it may be a mistake by the sculptor. (DEA PICTURE LIBRARY/De Agostini via Getty Images)

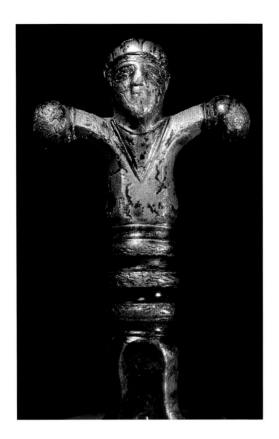

A Celtic 'anthropomorphic' sword hilt, so called because it is fashioned in the shape of a man. This example, dated to *c.*100 BC, was found in Ireland but was probably made in continental Europe. (Werner Forman/Universal Images Group/Getty Images)

Scapula then moved against Rome's enemies on the other side of the frontier. He led his army into the territory of the Deceangli in what is now north-west Wales, in what appears to have been a punitive expedition: his troops destroyed villages and burned crops and collected a great deal of booty. The Deceangli refused to meet the Romans in battle, however, opting instead to harass and ambush Scapula's troops on the march, further inciting them to ravage the Deceangli's lands. Scapula had almost reached the west coast when he was informed of unrest among the Brigantes, an allied tribe to the north of the province ruled by their queen Cartimandua, and was forced to turn back to contain it. Scapula wanted to secure the territory Rome had already conquered before he attempted to expand the frontiers of the province (Tacitus, *Annals* 32).

Caratacus and the Silures continued their incursions across the Severn. Scapula found that neither a policy of tolerance nor harshness would dissuade them from attacking, so he reinforced the western frontier with legionary strength. In order to free up a legion, he founded a colony of discharged Army veterans at Camulodunum, the former capital of the Catuvellauni and now the headquarters of the *legio XX*. The veterans were allocated their own areas of land to farm, and settled there with their families. Though discharged from regular service, the veterans would have remained as reservists, and maintained a strong Roman presence in the area, cultural as well as military. The *legio XX* was moved to a new fortress at Glevum (modern-day Gloucester), next to the southernmost crossing point on the Severn. From there, they could quickly move across the frontier, and penetrate deeply into Silurian territory by advancing up one of the many valleys running north to south into the uplands of what is now south Wales.

Scapula invaded the lands of the Silures to try to confront Caratacus. He commanded a powerful force of at least 20,000 men: as well as the *legio XX*, the *legio XIV* came down from Leicester and was likely reinforced by cohorts of the other two legions in the province, as well as a similar number of auxiliary infantry and cavalry (Webster 1981: 30). Tacitus tells us nothing of the campaign, other than that the Silures' natural fierceness was invigorated by the leadership of Caratacus, who more than compensated for his lack of military strength with an unparalleled use of the terrain to his tactical advantage. Caratacus refused to meet Scapula in open battle but instead withdrew northwards, into the increasingly mountainous and wooded country of the Ordovices. Here he brought together a large army, made up of his own retainers, those anti-Roman warriors who had followed him from elsewhere in the province, and Silurian and Ordovician tribesmen: as Tacitus described it, Caratacus' army was formed from 'all those who feared a Roman peace' (*Annals* 12. 33).

Roman military dagger (*pugio*) found at Hod Hill, a hillfort in southern Britain taken by the Romans soon after the invasion of AD 43. The sheath is decorated with geometric patterns inlaid with yellow brass. (© The Trustees of the British Museum)

MAP KEY

1 In the days leading up to the battle, Caratacus' army has occupied the high ground and built rough ramparts out of piles of stones to block the more accessible slopes.

2 When Scapula arrives he assembles his troops on the other side of the River Severn, and surveys the British defences.

3 Scapula leads the Roman infantry across the river. The legionaries and auxiliaries advance up the floor of the valley, where the British bombard them with javelins and rocks.

4 The Roman infantry assemble *testudo* formations and assault the ramparts.

5 After brutal hand-to-hand fighting, the Roman infantry breach the ramparts. The British retreat to the hilltops, pursued by the Roman infantry.

6 On the open ground, the unarmoured British tribesmen are overwhelmed by the Roman legionaries and auxiliaries. Many tribesmen are cut down, and others escape into the surrounding forests, including Caratacus himself.

Battlefield environment

Caratacus' last battle took place in the territory of the Ordovices, which stretched across much of what is now mid-Wales. It is not clear from Tacitus' account exactly where. Several hills in Wales and western England are called *Caer Caradoc*, which means 'Caratacus' fort'. Other sites are connected to Caratacus by local legend. Most of these are actually hillforts, which though they may have been occupied during the Roman invasion could not have been the site of the battle. Tacitus is clear that the British defences consisted only of hastily constructed stone ramparts: Caratacus' army did not defend an existing fort.

According to Tacitus, the battle took place above a river that was difficult to cross, most likely the River Severn. Webster (1981: 29) suggests that the battle was probably fought somewhere in the Severn valley around Caersws or Newtown in Powys, Wales. The Severn valley is narrow here, and many of the steep hills would fit Tacitus' brief description. Unfortunately, the course of the river has changed considerably over the centuries since the Roman invasion, and it is probably now impossible to locate the battlefield exactly.

A valley near Caersws above the River Severn in mid-Wales today. It is easy to see why the Roman legionary soldiers struggled to move and fight in this terrain. (Author)

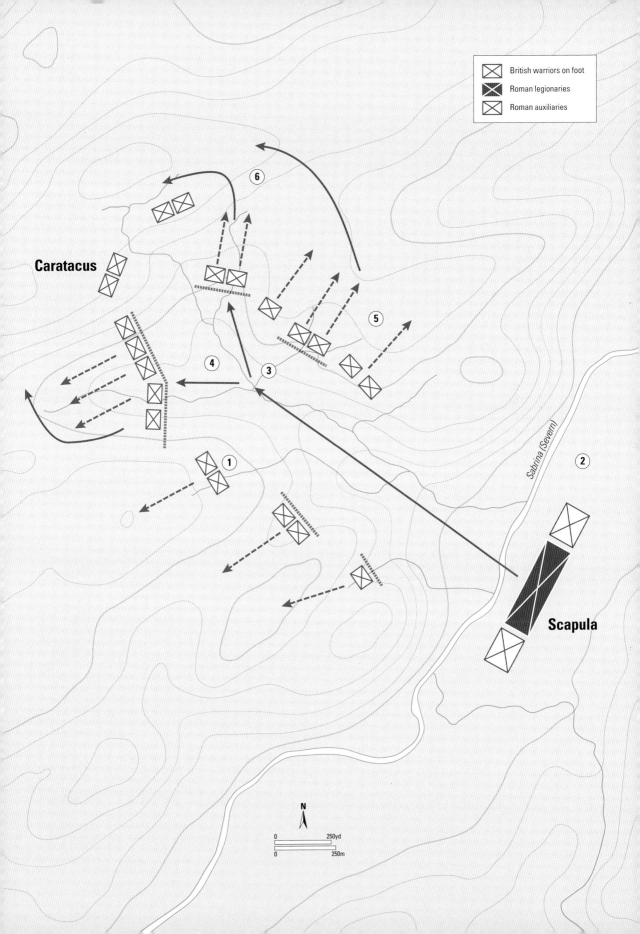

British warriors on foot
Roman legionaries
Roman auxiliaries

Caratacus

Scapula

Sabrina (Severn)

1
2
3
4
5
6

N

0   250yd
0   250m

INTO COMBAT

Caratacus knew he would have to fight Scapula eventually. His only hope of decisive victory against a Roman army lay in choosing a battlefield entirely favourable to his own forces. He found a site where his disparate bands of tribesmen could make full use of the terrain to make up for their lack of defensive armour: a narrow valley with precipitous sides. Here Caratacus' men would be out of reach of the disciplined ranks of Roman infantry and could attack from above with javelins and rocks, and the hillsides were surrounded by thick forest into which they could escape if necessary. At the bottom of the valley the British tribesmen were protected by a river without easy crossings, which would at least slow the Roman attack.

We do not have any first-hand accounts of this or any other battle between the British tribes and the Roman Army. We can, however, use the evidence we do have to reconstruct what it may have been like for the soldiers and warriors involved. After Caratacus had decided on the location of the battle, he ordered the construction of ramparts out of piles of stones, to prevent Roman infantry from advancing up the sides of the valley in those places where the terrain was not naturally so steep as to make it impossible. Presumably, this was done in the days preceding the battle, to ensure they were complete before the Romans discovered their location. The obvious advantages of their leader's choice of battlefield must have given the British a great deal of confidence. Many would have worked hard to dig up and move the boulders and rocks strewn across the hillsides to build the ramparts, looking forward to the battle in the belief they would be able to trap the Romans in the valley below. Others, particularly those members of the warrior elite who were used to riding into battle on their chariots before fighting hand to hand, may have been resentful of Caratacus' strategy, as it denied them the opportunity to demonstrate their bravery and commit exploits of personal heroism.

Scapula would have learnt of the British location from his cavalry scouts, who were undertaking constant patrols of the surrounding country. Tacitus tells us that when Scapula arrived in the valley, and first saw Caratacus' natural fortress, protected by the river and reinforced with stone bastions manned at every point by throngs of roaring British warriors, he was dismayed (*Annals* 12. 35). Caratacus and the other British leaders were moving among the tribesmen, shouting encouragement, firing their spirit, and inciting their enthusiasm for battle. Caratacus called upon the memory of their ancestors, who had routed Julius Caesar, and expelled his army from the shores of Britain. The British clamour grew louder, as every man swore an oath on his tribe that no weapons or wounds would make him yield.

Scapula hesitated. It is not surprising he was reluctant to commit his troops to what seemed like an impossible assault. He considered refusing to accept Caratacus' challenge and withdrawing, in the hope of catching up with the British in a more favourable location; but his soldiers were eager to fight, and exhorted their commander to attack, shouting that bravery would overcome any obstacle. Scapula discussed his plans with the commanding officers of the legions and the auxiliary cohorts. They shared their men's enthusiasm for battle. Scapula was won over by the fervour of his troops.

He made his own reconnaissance of the British positions, surveyed the river for crossings, and searched the hillsides and rocky defences for the most vulnerable points.

Scapula gave the order to attack. He led his forces across the river, which they crossed without difficulty. The Roman infantry filled the valley floor, and advanced like a huge piston being forced up to the top of a cylinder. The legions would have formed the vanguard, supported by auxiliary cohorts on either flank. They marched slowly, in near-silence. Only the shouts of the centurions could be heard above the rhythmic metallic clanking of the iron plates of the legionaries' armour, the jangling of their studded aprons, and the slapping of scabbards on thighs. Though frightened by the prospect of imminent combat, each legionary must have felt reassured that he was entering battle surrounded by the rest of his century: soldiers he had lived with, trained with and with whom he had endured years of brutal campaigning. He must also have been thankful for his weapons and equipment. Each legionary held his *scutum* in front of him with an overhand grip, the heavy shield protecting his body from knee to chin. His head was protected by an iron or copper-alloy helmet with a neck guard to deflect missiles and overhead blows, and his shoulders and torso were encased in flexible iron armour. In his right hand he carried his *pilum*, or heavy javelin, and his *gladius* was suspended from a belt on his right hip. Many legionaries also carried a *dolabra*, a soldier's pickaxe, which they would use to dismantle the enemy fortifications.

Caratacus

In the wake of Claudius' invasion of Britain, Caratacus was defeated in battle and fled westward, subsequently leading the Silures in a guerrilla campaign against the Roman Army. After Roman forces engaged Caratacus' men in battle, he led the defence of the British ramparts for as long as victory seemed possible. Caratacus is likely to have stayed well behind the front ranks, in an elevated position from where he could coordinate his forces. This would also have given him plenty of time in which to make his escape when it was clear that Scapula's infantry would breach the British bastions. Caratacus was so determined to get away that he even abandoned his wife and daughter. By the time of Caratacus' capture, tales of his exploits were well known in Rome (Tacitus, *Annals* 12.36). Perhaps Caratacus' greatest skill was survival. He managed to maintain his resistance for so long because he personally never stood his ground, never surrendered and, even when his army was defeated, always evaded capture.

Silver coin of Caratacus showing the British leader wearing an animal-skin headdress. An eagle with a snake in its talons is shown on the reverse. The first four letters of Caratacus' name, 'CARA', can be seen clearly on the obverse. Caratacus never understood the Romans' desire to enslave the world. After Claudius freed him, Caratacus reportedly wandered the streets of the imperial capital, and on seeing all the great and magnificent buildings, asked how a people who possessed so much could still covet the humble huts of his homeland (Cassius Dio, *Roman History* 60, 33). (© The Trustees of the British Museum)

The British must have presented an awesome sight. Screaming men covered the hilltops and ramparts, waving their weapons, shouting threats and boasting of their previous victories. The blaring whoops of the British *carnyces*, or war trumpets, with bells fashioned into the mouths of boars, serpents and mythical creatures, echoed around the valley; some had ornaments in the shape of wagging tongues or wide ears to make their impact more unsettling and terrifying. The British were dressed in woollen trousers, tunics and cloaks made from cloth woven in many colours, often with a striped or checked pattern. Their hair was long, as were their beards and luxurious, drooping moustaches. A number of warriors were naked or topless, their bodies covered in swirling, looping patterns in blue paint made from woad, and their hair was swept back and dressed into spikes, and streaked with lime. These warriors would have stood out in front, believing the magical properties of the woad designs would provide better protection than the cumbersome armour worn by the Romans.

The British were armed with a wide variety of weapons. Many brandished long, slashing swords and large oval or rectangular shields, painted with various designs; most carried spears, with long, elegant iron heads, and others clutched a handful of light javelins, or a sling and a bag of rocks, ready to rain down the missiles from their elevated positions on the hillside. Few would have been able to afford a coat of mail, or a helmet, though some would have proudly worn armour taken from the bodies of Roman soldiers. The ragtag army of Caratacus must also have included a great number of poorer men and boys who were armed only with stout sticks or clubs, farming tools or a knife.

The legionaries continued their relentless march uphill towards the ramparts. As the first cohorts approached, the British slingers would have begun the defensive effort, hurling small stones with the longest range. These would have struck the legionaries on the helmet, armoured shoulders and shields, and so would not have caused serious injury. Nevertheless, any soldier hit by a stone would have paused, breaking his step and slowing his unit's advance. The legionaries would have tried to dodge the stones, and deflect them with their shields. As the Romans moved closer, the British slingers would have selected larger stones, the size of a cricket ball, which could have disabled even an armoured legionary if it hit his head. A few yards further on, and the Romans entered the zone of maximum danger:

Publius Ostorius Scapula

Publius Ostorius Scapula was the son or grandson of Quintus Ostorius Scapula, who was one of the first Praetorian prefects, commanding the Praetorian cohorts that protected the Roman emperors. Nothing is known of Scapula's life before he arrived in Britannia as governor of the province in AD 47. He must have served as a consul, the highest magistracy in Rome, shortly before. Though we do not know anything of his prior military career, Scapula would have campaigned beforehand, probably as a legionary legate in command of a legion. Scapula led aggressive campaigns against Caratacus and the tribes of what is now Wales, particularly the Silures, who had begun a determined insurgency. He defeated and captured Caratacus in AD 50 but the Silures' insurrection continued. Scapula died of exhaustion in AD 51 while still in office. He may have been buried in Britain.

the British could now reach them with their javelins. They launched an unremitting attack from the hillsides and the stony embankments, using the natural advantage of height to cast their iron-tipped weapons onto the legionaries below. The Romans were in such close formations, the British did not even have to be accurate with their throws. The legionaries attempted to respond with their *pila*, but the British barrage was so ferocious that the Romans struggled to throw effectively, and they were severely hampered by the steepness of the ground.

The Romans were pinned, and many fell to the British missiles. For the legionaries in the centuries below the ramparts, forward progress must have seemed impossible. The order was given to form a *testudo*. We can imagine what it may have been like for the soldiers involved in the formation. The legionaries in the front ranks dropped to a crouch behind their shields, and closed the gaps between them, forming a solid wall. The soldiers behind lifted their heavy shields above their heads, and overlapped them slightly with those in the rank in front, so they slotted together like a tiled roof. Stones and javelins continued to hail down, banging and bouncing on the covering of shields. A few javelins penetrated, killing or wounding the legionary beneath, and some soldiers collapsed under the blow of a heavy rock. Only the front rank could see where they were going, and the soldiers behind began to trip and stumble on the uneven ground, as they struggled to keep their shields in place above their heads as the *testudo* edged forward.

At the rampart, several centurions broke out of the front rank, and led the assault. A swarm of legionaries followed. Many attempted to prise rocks away from the base and side of the fortifications with their pickaxes, the handles of their *pila*, or just their bare hands, while others drew their swords and stormed the bastion, hoping to push the British warriors back so their comrades could tear it down. The British flung themselves at the attacking legionaries, swinging their long swords in the air and slashing at the Romans' heads and shoulders, who caught the blows with the upper rim of their shields, and jabbed with their short, pointed swords at the Britons' exposed bellies. Other warriors thrust at the legionaries with their long-handled spears, just out of reach of the Romans' weapons. Some stood back and cast their javelins at short range, or picked up large rocks from the rampart and threw them at the legionaries. This was hand-to-hand combat at its most visceral. The Britons knew that the outcome of the battle depended on whether they could hold

Erected in 1894, this Victorian statue is reputed to represent Publius Ostorius Scapula, standing outside the Roman baths in the city of Bath in Somerset, south-west England. (Ad Meskens/ Wikimedia/CC BY-SA 3.0)

Contesting the rampart

The Roman *testudo* has reached the British rampart. A group of British warriors have run as fast as they could down the hillside from their elevated position to help defend the bastion. The Romans must not be allowed to breach the rampart, or the battle will be lost. A Roman centurion has courageously broken out of the front rank with a handful of legionaries, and is starting to dislodge some of the stones of the hastily built fortification with a *dolabra* (pickaxe). British warriors rush in, waving their long, slashing swords above their heads and raising their narrow-headed spears to cast at the Roman attackers. British missiles continue to hail down onto the Roman formation: rocks are banging onto the roof of interlocked shields, and javelins which fail to penetrate slide off with a rattle. Behind the rampart, a wall of legionaries crouch behind their shields, and try to shuffle forward to gain more ground. Two lift their shields above their heads and leap up onto the pile of stones to help protect the centurion from falling to British missiles, as another clears the rampart. A British swordsman dives forward to engage a legionary in single combat. These few minutes of furious confusion will decide the outcome of the battle.

the rampart, and the only way for the Romans to escape the British missiles was to take it.

Despite their courageous attempt to defend the fortification, the British were quickly overcome and fell back to the hilltops, followed by the Roman legionaries and auxiliary cohorts who poured through the breaches. As soon as the battle moved onto open ground the British lost all the advantages the terrain had given them. The Romans pressed forward in close formations, trapping the Britons between units of legionaries and auxiliaries. Here the British lack of helmets and armour left them completely at the mercy of

Fragment of a Roman glass relief, c.1st century AD, showing a pile of captured Celtic arms and armour. Several different shield types are visible, as well as helmets, a quiver of arrows and a boar-shaped standard. (metmuseum.org/CCO 1.0)

the Roman infantry, who crushed them between their disciplined ranks, constantly pushing with their shields and stabbing at the Britons' unprotected bodies and faces with their swords. As Tacitus records (*Annals* 12. 35), if the British tried to resist the auxiliaries they fell to the short swords and *pila* of the legionaries; if they turned to face these, they were cut down by the auxiliaries' long swords and spears. Many were captured, including Caratacus' wife and daughter and several of his brothers, but any tribesmen who were able to disappeared into the forests.

Caratacus himself escaped again, this time to the Brigantes, where he must have hoped to garner support to carry on the war. Queen Cartimandua remained loyal to the Romans, however, and arrested Caratacus and handed him over to them in chains. Caratacus and his family were taken to Rome, where they were paraded in front of Claudius along with the spoils of Scapula's campaign. Despite the cost to the empire of Caratacus' long resistance, Claudius pardoned him, and he and his family were allowed to live out their lives in the city of Rome, far from the forests and mountains of Britain.

Scapula had defeated Caratacus, but his victory did little to quell the western tribes' determination to continue the war. Soon after the battle, the Silures increased the intensity of their guerrilla campaign against the Roman Army. They ambushed troops constructing forts, killing many officers and men. In one engagement, the Silures attacked a foraging party, and routed the cavalry unit sent to rescue them. Scapula failed to dislodge the enemy with auxiliary infantry, and was only successful when he involved cohorts from the legions. The stress of the Silures' unrelenting offensive proved too much for Scapula, and he died of exhaustion while still in office, in AD 51.

Copper-alloy fittings from a set of segmented iron body armour of the type usually associated with Roman legionaries. The iron plates of the armour have not survived. Found at Hod Hill, a hillfort taken by the Romans after the invasion of Britain in AD 43. (© The Trustees of the British Museum)

The invasion of Mona

AD 60

BACKGROUND TO BATTLE

Scapula died during the winter of AD 51/52. He was succeeded as Roman governor of Britannia at some point in AD 52 by Aulus Didius Gallus, a very experienced general and administrator who had fought successful campaigns in the east of the Roman Empire and had even undertaken an expedition to the Crimea. Just as in the intervening months between the departure of Plautius and the arrival of Scapula, in the short period following Scapula's death when there was no governor present, the tribes to the west of the frontier took the opportunity to attack. The Silures crossed the Severn again and plundered Roman territory. A legion commanded by Gaius Manlius Valens, probably the *legio XX* based at Glevum, attempted to engage them and was embarrassingly defeated. The Silures continued to ravage Britannia until Gallus arrived with a stronger force and pushed them back (Tacitus, *Annals* 12.40).

The next region to erupt was the territory of the Brigantes. Cartimandua, queen of the Brigantes, divorced her husband Venutius after taking up with his shield bearer, Vellocatus (Tacitus, *Histories* 3.45). Humiliated, Venutius gathered an army to strike at both his former wife and the Romans. In response, Cartimandua captured Venutius' brother and other relatives, probably hoping to persuade Venutius to negotiate. Venutius instead invaded Cartimandua's kingdom with a band of picked warriors to attempt to free the hostages. Cartimandua was still a Roman ally, and appealed to Gallus, who dispatched an auxiliary force, which after an initial setback overcame the raiders. When a legion arrived under the command of Caesius Nasica, Venutius was defeated (Tacitus, *Annals* 12.40). Gallus made little further effort to expand the province westward and left Britannia in AD 57.

Detail of a Celtic shield found in Tal y Llyn Lake in north-west Wales. The three-pointed spiral design, known as a *triskeles*, is found on a number of Iron Age objects, though its meaning is unknown. (Werner Forman/Universal Images Group/Getty Images)

His replacement was Quintus Veranius, another able commander who had previously been governor of the province of Lycia and Pamphylia in Asia Minor, where he had crushed a coalition of mountain tribes. Unfortunately, Veranius died within a year.

Nero was keen to continue the conquest of the land now known as Wales. He sent Gaius Suetonius Paulinus, another 'mountain specialist', who had led a Roman army across the Atlas Mountains in Mauretania, to take over as governor (Dudley & Webster 1962: 49). Paulinus advanced across the western frontier into the territory of the Ordovices. For two years, Paulinus' column slowly ground its way through the forests and uplands of what is now north Wales, subduing the population and replacing their fortified settlements with auxiliary forts and legionary marching camps. Those British warriors who were determined to resist the Romans were forced further and further to the north and west, into the mountains of Snowdonia.

Paulinus knew how to fight in the mountains. He would have encircled the Snowdon massif, reducing any opposition before advancing into the mountains (Dudley & Webster 1962: 59). Yet Paulinus would have made slow progress. Even the navigable mountain passes would have been thickly forested and difficult for a large army to move through. The terrain perfectly suited the Ordovician tribesmen, who could travel undetected through the woods. They would have made the most of every opportunity to harass the Roman column, spring upon their foraging parties, and ambush units involved in the construction of forts and roads.

For the Roman legionaries in Paulinus' army, this must have been a stressful and frightening campaign. They never knew when an attack was coming, and they were at a severe disadvantage against an enemy employing such guerrilla tactics in this terrain. Their equipment – in particular, their large, curved, rectangular shields and heavy, jointed plate armour – and densely arrayed fighting style were best suited to combat with massed ranks of warriors in open battle. In these mountains, where the steep, forested hillsides prevented them from moving in their usual formations, they were forced to fight in a more open order, for which their equipment was unsuitable. Their shields were too large and unwieldy, and their short swords, so useful for stabbing at very close quarters, lacked the reach of the long, slashing swords of the British when fighting in small groups or skirmishes.

The Roman auxiliaries were much better suited to fighting in this environment. Their units were smaller, more flexible and more mobile than the legions, and their equipment was ideal for combat in 'open' formations against a dispersed and irregular enemy. Auxiliary infantry and cavalry soldiers of the 1st century AD were actually dressed and armed very much like elite Celtic warriors. They carried large, flat, oval shields with a central metal boss (*umbo*) covering a horizontal grip, and wore body armour made of mail (*lorica hamata*) or scale (*lorica squamata*), which was much more flexible than the banded iron armour (*lorica segmentata*) of the legionaries, and longer so it also protected the waist, groin and upper thighs. Their helmets were similar to those worn by legionaries (adapted from Celtic designs), though often of a simpler, cheaper style. Auxiliary cavalry, and possibly some infantry units, carried a long sword, known as a *spatha*, which was better for cutting and parrying than the legionaries' short, pointed *gladius*. In addition, the infantry carried one or more spears or javelins (*hastae*), and cavalry troopers were armed with a spear or lance (*lancea*). Auxiliaries in this period also wore woollen breeches or trousers like those worn by Celtic tribesmen, which were more practical in the cold and wet of north-west Britain than the legionaries' bare legs (Haynes 2013: 242–45).

After two years of difficult campaigning, Paulinus' determination and experience of mountain warfare paid off as the last of the Ordovices were driven out of their upland hideaways in Snowdonia. Soon their only place of refuge was the fertile and populous island of Mona (modern-day Anglesey), where a large army of displaced tribesmen began to gather. Mona was also the last stronghold of the druids, who the Romans were resolved to exterminate. Though they abhorred the druids' practice of human sacrifice, the Romans mostly feared the druids' power, which extended into all areas of British Celtic life. The druids not only controlled the British people's relationship with their gods, the natural world and each other; they had control over their life and death. In the Roman Empire, only the emperor and his appointed representatives had that power. If Britannia was ever going to become a peaceful Roman province, where the only law was Roman law, the druids would have to be wiped out (De La Bédoyère 2003: 56).

The Romans had other reasons for wanting to conquer the island of Mona. Unlike the nearby mainland, Mona was relatively flat and its fertile soils were well suited to agriculture. It was an ideal place to grow the wheat needed to feed the thousands of soldiers stationed in garrisons across what is now Wales. In addition, Mona contained significant deposits of copper,

Plaster cast of a scene from Trajan's Column, AD 113, showing Roman auxiliary soldiers defending a fortification. (Leemage/ Universal Images Group via Getty Images)

which indigenous tribes had been mining for thousands of years. Copper was very important to the Roman economy, and the Roman Army in particular. It was combined with zinc and tin to make much stronger copper alloys, which were used to manufacture military equipment such as helmets, shield bosses, and armour and belt fittings. Mona also occupied a strategic position on the north-west coast of what is now Wales. Possession of the island would have given the Romans control of all maritime traffic passing that part of the coast.

Paulinus prepared for an invasion. Though the Menai Strait, which separates the island from the mainland, is narrow – as little as 440yd wide in places – the tidal channel still presented a significant barrier. Although the Batavian cavalry had already proved that they could cross easily, getting thousands of Roman infantry soldiers over to the island was a major logistical challenge: Paulinus' army may have been as large as 25,000 men. It included two entire legions, the *legio XX* and the *legio XIV Gemina*, as well as detachments of others, and probably an equal number of auxiliaries (Dudley & Webster 1962: 59). Paulinus needed a coastal base from which to launch his invasion. Dudley and Webster (1967: 58) suggest that this was at Deva (modern-day Chester), which in the 1st century AD had a harbour accessible from the sea, and where a legionary fortress was built in AD 75. Paulinus would have summoned all available elements of the Roman Navy in Britain. He organized the construction of a fleet of flat-bottomed boats, which could carry his soldiers across the Menai Strait without becoming stranded in the shifting shallows (Tacitus, *Annals* 14.29).

MAP KEY

1 In the days before the invasion Plautius assembles his army on the mainland side of the strait. The legionary and auxiliary infantry embark upon a specially constructed fleet of flat-bottomed boats in the middle of the night. The British tribes on the island, their ranks swollen with thousands of refugees who have fled the Roman advance, flock to the shoreline.

2 In the half-light of dawn the Roman boats begin to cross the strait. Batavian auxiliary cavalry follow exposed sandbars and cross deeper channels by swimming alongside their horses.

3 On the beach, a ring of druids and black-clad priestesses scream curses and wave lit torches. The first Roman troops to land are paralysed with fear at the spectacle. Paulinus and his officers rally the Roman troops, who eventually advance up the beach.

4 The British rush to meet the invaders, but are cut down by the Roman infantry and soon turn and flee, pursued by the Roman cavalry.

Battlefield environment

We do not know where Paulinus' army crossed to Mona, nor where he mustered his forces for the embarkation. He would not necessarily have decided to cross the strait at the narrowest point, because the coast here slopes sharply towards the water, and many places would have been covered in a dense forest. Paulinus would probably have selected a landing site near the western entrance to the strait, where the beaches are wide and gently sloping, and where the more level terrain would have enabled his troops to move inland quickly.

The crossing was dangerous. The tide rises at different rates through the two entrances to the strait, causing unpredictable currents, and it is criss-crossed with wide banks of soft mud and sand. The marines crewing the Roman boats would have had to pick their route carefully, so they did not become trapped among the treacherous shoals. Likewise, the Batavian officers leading the cavalry units must have looked for the safest fords.

The mountains of Snowdonia as they are today. It is easy to imagine the Roman armies of Paulinus and Agricola struggling through these steep-sided valleys, searching for the elusive warriors of the Ordivices. (Author)

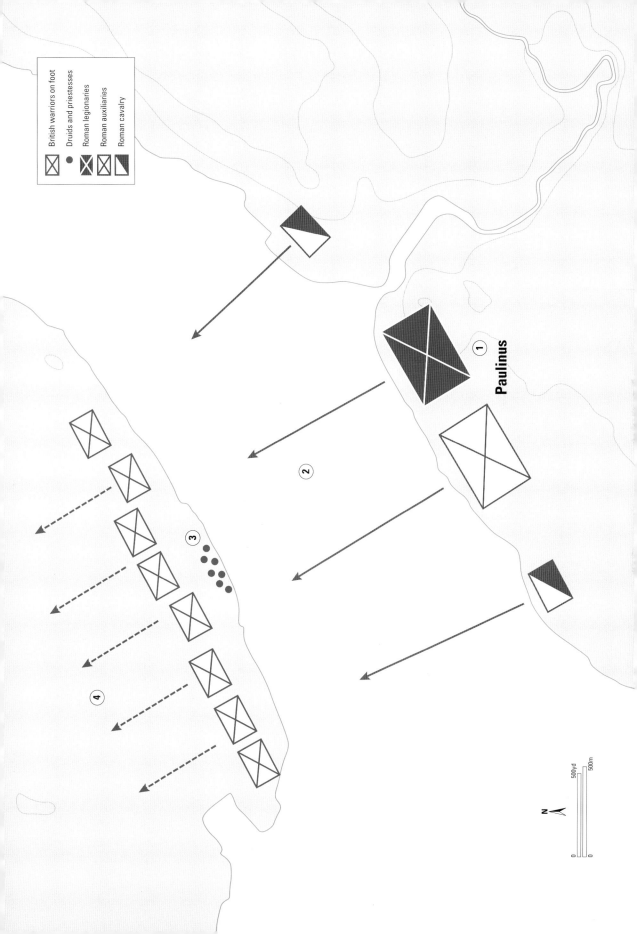

Paulinus

British warriors on foot
Druids and priestesses
Roman legionaries
Roman auxiliaries
Roman cavalry

1

2

3

4

N

500yd
500m

INTO COMBAT

We only have one literary source for the invasion. Tacitus described the battle in brief but vivid detail in his *Annals of Imperial Rome* (14.29–30). Tacitus was not present at the battle, but it is very likely that his father-in-law, Gnaeus Julius Agricola, was, as he served as a military tribune on Paulinus' staff at this time (Tacitus, *Agricola*: 5). We can assume, therefore, that Agricola told Tacitus what had happened. Unfortunately, Tacitus did not record who was in command of the British on Mona, if there was any individual at all leading the indigenous people and the multifarious mixture of warriors and tribesmen who had gathered there. The island had become a haven for refugees from the rest of Britain. Many would have fled to Mona with their families, or perhaps a wider tribal group, hoping to find there a place where they could continue to live as they had done before the Romans arrived. Others had fought the Romans repeatedly in the mountains and forests, and had retreated in the face of relentless pressure from the Roman Army. Some may have moved there believing the druids would protect them from the foreign invaders. All must have been dismayed to hear that the Romans were heading for their sanctuary by land and sea.

In the early summer of AD 60 Paulinus must have advanced from Deva. He most likely led his army along the coast, and across the River Conwy, to the shore of the Menai Strait. The Roman naval vessels, towing the flotilla of flat-bottomed boats out at sea, would have kept pace with the troops on land. When Paulinus reached the coast opposite Mona, he would have organized his forces prior to embarkation. Roman engineers would have surveyed the beaches and bays for the best place to load the legionaries and auxiliary infantry into the boats, and calculated when the tide was suitable for them and the cavalry to cross. The first Roman troops would likely have embarked at night, ready to cross at daybreak. Darkness would have hidden their preparations on the mainland and the dawn half-light would have been just enough to navigate the tricky crossing while hopefully preserving the element of surprise. We can imagine what it must have been like for the infantry soldiers crammed together between the banks of rowers in the hulls

Copper-alloy Roman helmet found in the River Thames in London, c.1st century AD. The cheek guards have been lost. This helmet has the names of four different Roman soldiers punched into the underside of the neck guard. Roman soldiers had to pay for their own armour and weapons, which could be very expensive, so there was clearly a ready market for second-hand military equipment. (© The Trustees of the British Museum)

of the boats. They would have been afflicted by seasickness and apprehensive that their boats would capsize: even if they were able to swim, few soldiers could have done so for long in a metal helmet and iron armour.

The auxiliary cavalry would probably have ridden in narrow files along the sandbanks. The troopers would likely have strapped their shields and lances to the left side of their horses' saddles but were otherwise ready for battle in their mail armour and helmets. When they reach a channel too deep for their horses to wade, the troopers would have dismounted and led their horses into the water with a short rein, twisting the other hand into the leather strap of the saddle as the horses began to swim. As they urged their mounts forward, the troopers would have had to kick furiously to keep afloat in their heavy armour. When the animals' feet touched the seabed again, the troopers would have swung themselves back into the saddle.

As soon as they heard that Paulinus' army was approaching, the British would have commenced preparations to defend the island. Bands of warriors must have camped near the coast, ready to rush to wherever the Romans chose to land. On the night that Paulinus' army began to clamber into their boats, perhaps spies slipped across the channel to warn the British, or sent signals by lighting beacons in the darkness. In any event, the British knew the Romans were coming. According to Tacitus, as the Romans boats and swimming cavalry crossed the strait, a dense swarm of armed warriors already lined the shore (*Annals* 14.30).

The warriors were not alone. Among them ran black-clad women with dishevelled hair – presumably some kind of priestesses – waving flaming torches. In front, a circle of druids stood with their arms thrust up to the sky, bringing down frightful curses. The presence of the priestesses and druids on the beach must have given the massed British warriors formidable confidence. Thousands of men were shouting and singing, waving their weapons, banging their swords and spears against their shields, threatening and challenging the approaching Romans. The entire beach reverberated with a great cacophony

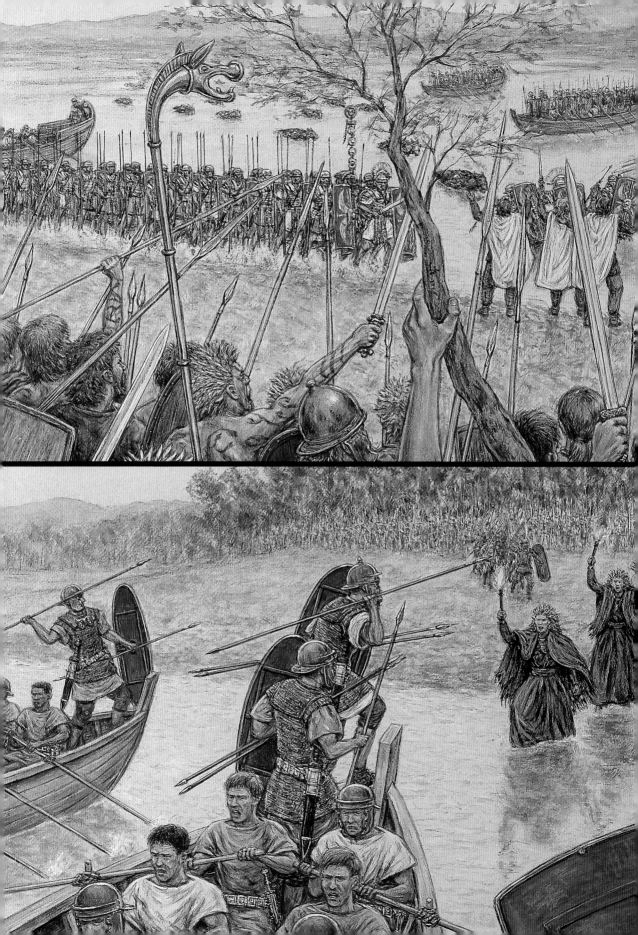

Moving to contact on the beaches of Mona

British Celtic view: As the light slowly returned over the narrow strait between the island of Mona and the mainland, word reached the British camps that the Roman army was crossing. A young boy, a refugee from the Ordovices whose family fled to Mona after their hillfort home was taken and destroyed by Paulinus' troops, has hidden among the branches of a tall tree. Here he can watch his kinsmen finally take their revenge on the hated Roman soldiers who have occupied his tribes' land. The British force has massed among the trees lining the beach, where they wait, ready to drive the invaders back into the water. A group of druids stand in the shallows, their arms thrust toward the sky, and black-clad priestesses brandish flaming torches and scream horrifying curses. Their presence has buoyed the British defenders, whipping them into a frenzy of boasting and roaring. As the first Roman boats slide to a stop in the soft sand, the British clash their weapons against their shields, whoop and holler, and the shrill blare of their *carnyces* echoes among the trees.

Roman view: Having embarked in the darkness, 20 fully armoured soldiers crouch unsteadily in the black hull of each flat-bottomed boat. Every vessel is crewed by 12 marines, who haul on their creaking oars in unison to the call of the helmsmen, whose voices can only just be heard floating over the sound of clanking armour, the knock of shields against the bulwarks, and the rush of the wind and the sea. Between the boats, horses swim, their noses nodding high out of the spray, as their Batavian riders cling to their saddles and bridles, kicking with their legs to stay afloat in their heavy armour. A centurion has leapt from the first boat to land. Behind him, a legionary steps onto the prow and raises his heavy *pilum*, ready to cast. He is about to jump down into the surf when he catches sight of the druids on the beach, and hears the wails and curses of the priestesses. He is suddenly paralysed, petrified by the fear of what these wicked magicians might do to him. In front, his centurion screams a battle cry and orders him forward, and the soldiers behind encourage him not to fear a mob of raving women. Muttering a prayer, he prepares himself to drop into the water and advance up the beach.

of voices and the noise from *carnyces* echoed among the trees lining the beach. As the Romans came closer to the island shore, the British slingers, stone-throwers and javelineers would have hurried down the beach, ready to bombard the Romans as they scrambled to disembark from their flat-bottomed boats.

The sight of the druids and black-clad priestesses had the opposite effect on the Roman soldiers. Tacitus tells us (*Annals* 14.30) that many were so frightened by the druids' curses and the weird spectacle of the crazed women that they were rooted to the spot, as if gripped by some kind of paralysis. To the Romans, the women looked like furies, goddesses of vengeance who rose from the underworld to punish those who broke oaths or committed serious crimes; and all would have feared the murderous magic of the druids. The Romans were so intimidated that they could not move from the beach. Exposed in the surf and open sand in front of the empty boats, they were completely at the mercy of the British missiles. Javelins and rocks pelted down on the legionaries and auxiliaries, and many were wounded. Paulinus, who would have landed in the first wave of Roman boats, urged his men forward. He exhorted them not to fear a rabble of women and fanatics, while centurions and fellow soldiers shouted similar encouragements to those still overcome with fear. Roman discipline and training quickly prevailed. The soldiers huddling along the shore began to form up into centuries and cohorts, and they raised and interlocked their shields to protect themselves and each other from the British missiles. Paulinus ordered the Roman standards to the front and the blare of Roman trumpets sang across the sand. The Roman army advanced up the beach.

Unfortunately, Tacitus gives little detail about the rest of the battle, but we can reconstruct what might have happened based on our knowledge of Roman and Celtic tactics. Keeping strict formation, and marching silently in step, the legionaries and auxiliary infantry pressed forward towards the British horde. The cavalry most likely stayed back in reserve. As the Romans approached, the British rushed forward to meet them,

ABOVE LEFT
Dating from the 1st century AD, this is the tombstone of Vonatorix, who served as an auxiliary cavalryman in the *ala Longiniana*. His 'scale' armour is clearly depicted, as is his long cavalry sword, known as a *spatha*. Now in the Rheinisches Landesmuseum Bonn, Germany. (DeAgostini/Getty Images)

ABOVE RIGHT
Detail of a funerary stele dated to *c.*AD 80 and erected in honour of Marcus Aemilius Durises, a cavalryman in the *ala Sulpicia*. This section shows a groom attending to Durises' horse. His shield is attached to the left and side of the saddle, and the horse's tack is clearly depicted. (DEA/G. DAGLI ORTI/Getty Images)

bellowing their battle cries and hurling their javelins at their resolutely silent opponents. Despite the fearsome British noise and missile attack, the Romans waited until they were within about 50ft of their enemy before the legionaries launched their own javelins (Goldsworthy 2011: 184). The legionaries' heavy *pila* were particularly effective, as their extra weight helped them to penetrate the British warriors' shields, causing the thin, iron shanks to bend. The bent *pila* were very hard to remove from the shields, making them impossibly heavy and unwieldy. The warriors were forced to throw their shields aside, leaving themselves completely unprotected as few wore armour. Those *pila* that missed their targets often bent anyway when they hit the ground, so they were useless to the British warriors.

As soon as the Romans had released their javelin volley, they drew their swords from the scabbards on their right hips. Raising their own battle cry, they charged the last few yards to smash into the British ranks (Goldsworthy 2011: 184). The British swung their long, round-tipped swords in huge, powerful arcs, bringing them down with brutal force on the Roman soldiers' heads and shoulders. The Romans crouched behind their raised shields, which they held side by side to protect themselves and each other. They tried to catch the vicious British blades with the reinforced rims of their shields. The centurions ordered the soldiers onward, and they pushed their shield wall forward into the furious, flailing British swordsmen. The British were squashed against their own ranks, where they had little space to raise their shields and swing their long swords. As the Romans pressed relentlessly forward, they flicked and jabbed their short, pointed swords through the thin gaps between their shields, into the exposed bodies and faces of the British. Without space to use their long weapons, the British were quickly forced back. The rear ranks gave way first, and many turned and fled.

This was exactly what the Roman cavalry were waiting for. As the British resolve broke, and warriors started to fall back, the cavalry dashed after them. They galloped between the fleeing tribesmen, spearing them with their light lances, or cutting them down with their long-bladed swords. The cursing druids and shrieking priestesses likely met the same fate. Tacitus records only that the enemy was engulfed in a fire lit with their own torches (*Annals* 14.30).

Paulinus immediately began to subdue the island of Mona. He set up garrisons and forts and set about dismantling the power of the druids. Roman soldiers destroyed the druids' sacred groves, and tore down the altars which they had soaked with the blood of their sacrificial victims. Paulinus had conquered the last stronghold of the druids, and the Roman Army now controlled most of what is now north Wales. Unfortunately, Paulinus was not able to enjoy his victory for long. While he and half the Roman troops stationed in Britain had been away on campaign, the south-eastern part of Britannia had erupted in the most ferocious rebellion. Paulinus gathered his army and marched south-east as fast as his men could move. Boudicca's uprising had begun.

Although Paulinus defeated Boudicca's rebel army in a single, decisive battle, the uprising did a great deal of damage to Britannia. The British rebels destroyed the veteran colony at Camulodunum established by Scapula, and sacked the towns of Verulamium (St Albans) and Londinium (London). The Roman army also suffered. The *legio IX* lost so many men to a rebel ambush that Nero had to send 2,000 legionaries from Germany to bring it back up to strength, accompanied by eight auxiliary infantry cohorts and a cavalry *ala*. Boudicca's uprising and its brutal suppression by Paulinus also severely damaged relations between the native Britons and their Roman rulers. Civil unrest continued to plague Britannia for the rest of the year, fuelled by famine. British tribesmen in Boudicca's army had spent the summer away from their villages, neglecting their farms, and they had not returned in time to harvest their produce. Roman troops also burned the crops and destroyed the livestock of hostile and neutral tribes (Tacitus, *Annals* 14.31–38).

Nero replaced Paulinus with Publius Petronius Turpilianus, whose mild rule quietly extinguished the last embers of rebellion. Turpilianus

A life-sized bronze head thought to represent the emperor Claudius. It was violently torn from the rest of the statue, and deposited in the River Alde near Saxmundham in Suffolk. This may be a relic of the Iceni uprising of AD 60, led by Boudicca. When the head was found in 1907, scholars suggested that it could have been an imperial portrait that once adorned a public building at Camulodunum, which was removed when the veteran colony was sacked by Boudicca's rebels and carried back to Iceni territory as a trophy. (CM Dixon/Print Collector/Getty Images)

was in turn succeeded by Marcus Trebellius Maximus, who also concentrated on the civilian administration of Britannia, rather than military campaigns across its frontiers. The next governor, Marcus Vettius Bolanus, achieved little (Tacitus, *Agricola* 16). The British leader Venutius seized the opportunity to again attack the Brigantian queen Cartimandua, whose kingdom stretched across the northern border of Britannia. Bolanus did not have the resources to defeat Venutius, however, and left him holding the Brigantian throne (Tacitus, *Histories* 3.45).

Nero's successor as emperor, Vespasian (r. AD 69–79), was determined to expand the frontiers of Britannia and appointed Quintus Petilius Cerialis, an experienced and able general, as governor. Cerialis had been the commander of the *legio IX* when it was savaged by Boudicca's rebels, and had recently put down a revolt of the Batavians on the Rhine. On taking office, Cerialis immediately attacked the Brigantes, and after several bloody battles, he presumably defeated Venutius, and brought much of Cartimandua's former kingdom under direct Roman control (Campbell 2010: 13). Cerialis was followed by another effective military governor, Sextus Julius Frontinus, who advanced across the lower Severn and finally subjugated the Silures (Tacitus, *Agricola* 17). Frontinus left Britannia in AD 77. His successor was Gnaeus Julius Agricola.

Mons Graupius

AD 83

BACKGROUND TO BATTLE

In midsummer AD 77 Gnaeus Julius Agricola took over as governor of Britannia. He had fought in Britain before as a tribune under Paulinus during Boudicca's rebellion, and had later returned to Britain to command the *legio XX* under the later governor Quintus Petilius Cerialis. As had happened so many times in the past, in the short period before Agricola landed in Britannia, tribes in what is now Wales attacked Roman forces stationed there. The Ordovices almost destroyed a cavalry unit and ripples of unrest began

Detail of the neck guard of a Celtic copper-alloy helmet, *c.*150–50 BC, found in the River Thames. It is decorated with typical Celtic swirling designs. The scored 'buttons' would once have held coloured enamel. (Werner Forman/Universal Images Group/Getty Images)

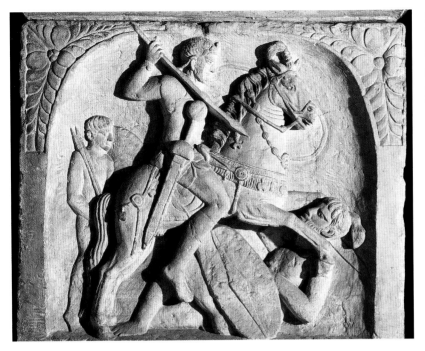

Dating from the late 1st century AD, this detail is from the tombstone of Titus Flavius Bassus, an auxiliary cavalryman in the *ala Noricum*. (DEA/A. DAGLI ORTI/De Agostini via Getty Images)

to spread (Tacitus, *Agricola* 18). By the time Agricola had travelled to the region, summer was nearly over. The Ordovices, and much of his own army, had assumed there would be no campaigning that year. Agricola thought otherwise. Overcoming his soldiers' inertia, he led a combined legionary and auxiliary force into the mountains of north Wales, and caught the Ordovices by surprise. Tacitus reports (*Agricola* 18) that almost the whole population was slaughtered.

The new governor continued his lightning campaign. He struck at once towards Mona, resolved to finish the conquest of the island begun by Paulinus. Agricola had probably been present at the first invasion, and was confident he could repeat Paulinus' success. He did not have time to construct a fleet of boats to ferry the infantry over the Menai Strait, however. Instead, Agricola relied entirely on the amphibious skills of his Batavian cavalry, whom he ordered across to the island so suddenly that the British warriors living there were completely caught out. They had assumed that they would have had significant warning of any new Roman assault, as the Roman army and fleet would have needed time to assemble. The British leaders on Mona saw there was little to be gained from further resistance and surrendered (Tacitus, *Agricola* 18).

When winter finally arrived, Agricola turned his attention to Britannia. He understood that the province would never be peaceful until the British people accepted Roman rule. Agricola reorganized the provincial administration, beginning with his own household, and instructed his subordinates to treat the British, even in recently conquered territory, with leniency. He reformed the tax system and rooted out corruption. Agricola realized that the British needed to see the benefits of their incorporation into the Roman Empire. He assisted communities to build Roman amenities such as temples, marketplaces and baths, and encouraged loyal members of the elite to build Roman-style houses, adopt Roman costume, and send their sons to him to be given a

Roman education. Tacitus records (*Agricola* 21) that Agricola's campaign to 'Romanize' Britannia was so successful that the British were soon led astray by the 'evils' of Roman urban culture, hot baths and dinner parties.

Military campaigning continued. In AD 79 Agricola advanced northwards, and completed Cerialis' pacification of the coalition of tribes in Brigantia. He then led his army on an expedition even further to the north, and reached the *Taus*, the River Tay in southern Scotland. The tribe in this area, probably the Dumnonii (Campbell 2010: 41), had not yet encountered the Romans. Despite being aided by damaging storms that hindered the Romans' progress, they were overwhelmed. Agricola's troops built a series of forts in which they were able to remain for the winter, and dominate the locality (Tacitus, *Agricola* 22).

Agricola spent the next summer consolidating his gains. He withdrew to a new frontier where the wide estuaries of the *Clota* and the *Bodotria* (now known as the Firths of Clyde and Forth respectively) reach far inland to a create a natural 'bottleneck', and secured the region with garrisons (Tacitus, *Agricola* 23). His army then turned west, and invaded the territory of the Novantae amid what are now called the Galloway Hills (Campbell 2010: 45). Tacitus describes (*Agricola* 24) how Agricola assembled his troops along the shore facing Ireland and briefly considered an invasion. The following year, AD 82, Agricola summoned the Roman Navy. As his troops overtook communities living north of the *Bodotria*, the Navy and Army worked closely together, advancing at the same time by sea and land. Tacitus mentions (*Agricola* 25) that soldiers from the infantry and cavalry often shared the same camp with sailors. Agricola himself even sailed ahead to survey the coast for natural harbours, in case hostile tribes attempted to block the land route northwards. Captured prisoners revealed to Agricola that the local tribes were amazed by the sight of the Roman fleet, because it meant that their hidden coastal strongholds were now no longer safe.

The Roman Army had entered Caledonia. We know very little about the inhabitants of this vast area, which Tacitus implies covered the whole of northern Britain above Agricola's new frontier between the estuaries of the *Clota* and *Bodotria*. The population of the region lived in loosely affiliated tribal groups, in small, dispersed settlements. Cassius Dio recorded (*Roman History* 77.12) a much later expedition into Caledonia by the Roman emperor Septimius Severus (r. AD 193–211) in AD 208. He described the local tribespeople as living in wild and swampy wastes, where they dwelled in 'tents'. They did not grow crops but subsisted on flocks of sheep, wild game and fruits, and mostly went about naked. Their society was democratic but as they enjoyed raiding the settlements of other tribes, they chose strong men to lead them. In battle, the Caledonians made use of chariots, which were pulled by small, fast horses. Most fought as infantry, carrying shields, daggers and spears with a bronze 'apple' on the end that the warriors would bang against their shields to make a terrifying noise. The Caledonians were tough fighters, who would hold their ground. Another Roman historian, Herodian, describing the same campaign (*History* 3.14.7–8), added that these savage warriors also painted their naked bodies with coloured patterns and images of animals and wore jewellery made of iron. In addition to their shields and spears, they carried swords suspended from a belt around their naked waists. Tacitus notes that the Caledonians' swords were 'enormous' and their shields 'small' (*Agricola* 36), and they had red-gold hair and strong limbs (*Agricola* 11).

The Caledonians banded together to repel the Roman Army. Tribesmen came from all over the region to join the growing British force, which first attacked some of the Roman forts. These surprise assaults caused a great deal of alarm within Agricola's army. Several of his officers tried to persuade Agricola to withdraw his troops to the *Bodotria* before he was driven there by the Britons, who were approaching in a number of 'warbands'. Agricola realized that his army risked being encircled by what Tacitus described as a 'superior force' (*Agricola* 25), who were obviously familiar with the terrain. To avoid this, he split his army into three groups, and continued to advance. The Britons would have been following the Romans' movements closely. They quickly identified the weakest of the three Roman columns, which was formed by the *legio IX* and a number of auxiliary cohorts. The British attacked at night while the Romans were inside their marching camp. They stole up to the gates, and after killing the sentries, broke into the camp and spread panic among the sleeping soldiers. The fighting was fierce in the darkness. Fortunately for the legionaries of the *legio IX*, Agricola had been closely tracking the Caledonian force. He ordered his fastest cavalry and infantry units to press ahead, and at first light they charged into the attackers' rear. The British were trapped, and fought savagely to break out through the gates of the camp. The combined Roman force prevailed and the British were routed. Many were able to escape into the safety of the marshes and forests (Tacitus, *Agricola* 26).

Agricola's soldiers were emboldened by their victory. They urged their commander to push on into Caledonia and, even if they had to fight battle after battle, finish the conquest of the whole of Britain. Winter was approaching, however, and Agricola returned to his line of forts on the frontier, where he began to plan the next summer's campaign. The Britons were just as determined to resist the Roman invaders, and continued to prepare for war. They moved their families to safety and armed even the youngest men. Different tribes met and strengthened their alliances with sacrifices. In Caledonia, the British tribes had finally realized that the Romans were a danger to all, and they could only be beaten if the tribes came together to form a united army (Tacitus, *Agricola* 29).

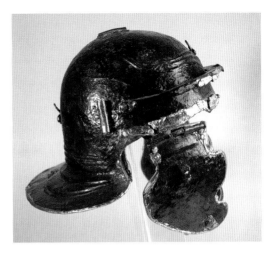

Dating from the 1st century AD, this Roman helmet was found in the amphitheatre in Besançon, France. The brow reinforcement and deep neck guard gave excellent protection against the typical downward sword strokes of Celtic enemies. (DEA/G. DAGLI ORTI/De Agostini via Getty Images)

Roman short sword (*gladius*) found in the River Thames at Fulham in London. The shape of the blade, often referred to as the 'Mainz' type, has a long, tapering point for stabbing, and was popular in the first half of the 1st century AD. The ornate scabbard is decorated with scenes of hunting and the lives of Romulus and Remus. (© The Trustees of the British Museum)

MAP KEY

1. The Caledonian army has gathered over several days on the plain at the foot of Mons Graupius. Having learnt of their location, Agricola has built a large fortified camp nearby. On the morning of the battle, the Caledonian infantry have spread out in long lines across the mountainside. The front ranks occupy the edge of the plain, where chariots career up and down. Leaving his legions and four *alae* of cavalry in reserve in front of the Roman camp, Agricola advances with cohorts of auxiliary infantry and cavalry.

2. Agricola orders the cohorts to open their ranks to prevent the larger Caledonian force from outflanking them, and closes to within missile range. The two sides exchange javelins.

3. Agricola commands the Batavian and Tungrian cohorts to engage the British in hand-to-hand combat. The auxiliary cavalry drive the British chariots from the field.

4. The rest of the Roman auxiliary infantry engages, and the Romans begin to push up the slope. The auxiliary cavalry attack the Caledonian lines and become trapped in the difficult terrain.

5. The Caledonian infantry stationed further up the mountainside begin to descend and try to move around the rear of the Roman auxiliary infantry.

6. Agricola orders the four *alae* to gallop up the slope to intercept the Caledonian reinforcements, who turn and flee.

7. The Roman cavalry swing round and charge the remaining Caledonian tribesmen from the rear. The Caledonian line breaks and the fleeing tribesmen are cut down by the cavalry as they try to escape into the surrounding forests.

Battlefield environment

Historians and antiquarians have searched for the location of Mons Graupius for centuries. Tacitus does not describe the location of the mountain in his *Life of Agricola*, but it is possible to gather some clues from within the text. It appears to have been a high, ridged mountain, which stood above a flat plain, somewhere in northern Scotland. Some historians have attempted to analyse the name 'Graupius' itself, and have argued that it is derived from a Celtic word which may describe the physical characteristics of the mountain or relate to its modern name (Fraser 2008: 72–78). Others have searched for evidence of a nearby Roman marching camp that would fit Tacitus' narrative. The famous British archaeologist Kenneth St Joseph, who pioneered the use of aerial photography to survey ancient sites, discovered the remains of the largest Roman camp yet known in northern Scotland at Durno, near Inverurie in Aberdeenshire in 1975 (St Joseph 1978: 271-287). He argued that a camp of such a size would have been built to accommodate an unusually large force, mustered for a special operation. This could only have been Agricola's army encamped in readiness to meet the assembled Caledonian tribal army at Mons Graupius. A high, isolated hill called Bennachie lies only 1.8 miles from Durno, and it dominates the skyline from the camp. In front of Bennachie is an open plain, large enough to have been the battlefield, and it is easy to imagine the Caledonian horde massed in long lines across the curving hillside. Unfortunately, no physical evidence of the battle has been found, such as weapons, armour or bones, but Bennachie remains the most likely site of the battle (Campbell 2010: 91–92).

A woad plant (*Isatis tinctoria*). Woad was used to produce a blue dye to colour textiles and as a body paint or ink for tattoos. Julius Caesar recorded (*Gallic Wars* 5.14) that the people of Britain painted themselves with woad to make themselves look frightening. (DEA/E. MARTINI/De Agostini via Getty Images)

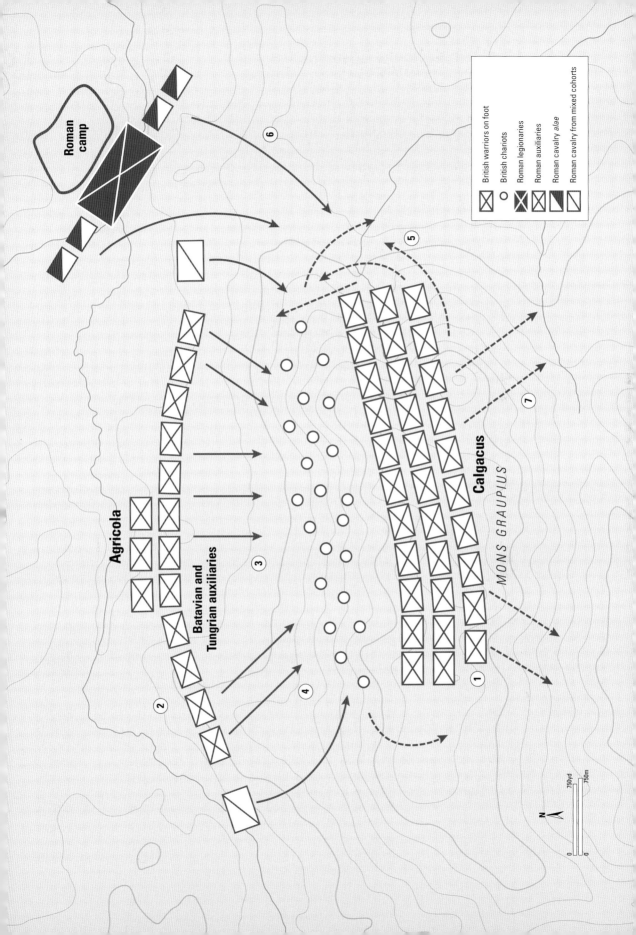

Roman camp

Agricola

Batavian and
Tungrian auxiliaries

② ③ ④

①

Calgacus

MONS GRAUPIUS

⑤ ⑥ ⑦

British warriors on foot

British chariots

Roman legionaries

Roman auxiliaries

Roman cavalry *alae*

Roman cavalry from mixed cohorts

N

0   750yd

0   750m

INTO COMBAT

Campaigning began again the next summer, in AD 83. As soon as the weather allowed, Agricola dispatched the Roman fleet. His ships attacked British settlements around the coast, spreading panic and uncertainty among the Caledonian tribes (Tacitus, *Agricola* 29). Agricola marched northwards, determined to find and destroy the swelling Caledonian tribal army. He commanded a powerful force, augmented with British units raised from loyal tribes in the south of Britannia. He forced his men to travel with minimal equipment, so they could move faster through the forests and swamps. The British would have constantly harassed the Roman column, ambushing scouts and foraging parties, and raiding their marching camps. Tacitus records (*Agricola* 33) that Agricola's exhausted men often asked their commander to tell them when they would find their enemy, and when they would finally have the chance to meet them in battle.

The British clearly felt the same. The Caledonian leaders knew that their only hope of preventing their territory from being swallowed up by the relentless expansion of the Roman Empire was to defeat the Roman Army in pitched battle. Just like Caratacus more than 30 years earlier, the British chose a location for their 'last stand' where the terrain would be entirely to their own advantage. Sometime in late summer AD 83, the Caledonian tribes gathered on the slopes of a high, many topped hill, which Tacitus called *Mons Graupius*, or 'the Graupian Mountain'. Warbands from all over Caledonia joined the tribal army. When news reached Agricola that the British were massing for battle, it was reported that more than 30,000 men could be seen, and more warriors were continuing to arrive (Tacitus, *Agricola* 29). Agricola ordered his lightly equipped army to advance to Mons Graupius, where they constructed a well-defended marching camp close to the foot of the hill, in full view of the massing British horde.

The Caledonians had many leaders. The army encamped on the steep slopes of Mons Graupius was made up of tribal groups of all sizes, drawn from a very wide territory. Each group would have been led by a member of the local warrior elite who through longstanding ties of kinship, or recently formed alliance, may have sworn allegiance to another, more powerful warrior. In this way, a large fighting force was quickly recruited. Tacitus records (*Agricola* 29) that at Mons Graupius, a leader had emerged called Calgacus, who was outstanding among all others for his nobility and bravery. No other mention is made of this 'Calgacus', which some scholars suggest might be a title rather than a name, because 'Calgacus' may mean 'swordsman'. Just as the British tribes in what is now Wales had joined forces under the leadership of Caratacus, the Caledonians appear to have proclaimed a single general (Campbell 2010: 33).

Calgacus addressed the assembled British tribesmen. The words of the stirring speech that Tacitus records the chieftain making are almost certainly Tacitus' own, but the sentiment must have been the same. Calgacus reminded the Caledonian warriors that they were Britain's last defence. All other tribes and territories had already fallen under the Roman yoke. If they failed to defeat the Roman Army on that day, they and their families would become Roman slaves, just like the rest of the population of Britain. Calgacus pointed

Iron spear-head of the type used by both Celtic and Roman auxiliary troops in the 1st century AD. (Universal History Archive/Universal Images Group via Getty Images)

down at the Roman soldiers, formed up inside their fortified camp. Unlike them, he told them, the Romans did not have wives there to galvanize them, or parents to scold them if they ran away. The Romans were all far from home, in a strange and inhospitable country, and many of the Roman soldiers were themselves aliens, serving a foreign army put together from very different peoples. The Roman Army was only held together by success. Calgacus assured the British tribesmen that defeat would cause it to fall apart (Tacitus, *Agricola* 30–32).

The British tribesmen erupted. Singing, shouting and pounding their weapons, they spread out across the high slopes of Mons Graupius. The Roman troops, assembled behind the earthen rampart that surrounded their marching camp, watched as the British formed a series of long, thick lines of infantry on the mountainside. The bravest warriors moved out in front and occupied the edge of the flat ground at the foot of the mountain, where they screamed challenges and taunts at the Romans. On the open plain in front a large number of Caledonian chariots careered up and down. The charioteers showed off their incredible horsemanship as their light vehicles bounced over the wet, uneven ground, and the elite warriors they carried brandished their weapons (Tacitus, *Agricola* 35). From across the slope, the furious British din and the eerie sounds from animal-headed *carnyces* floated down to the Roman camp. The British did all they could to intimidate and alarm their enemy.

Detail of the central roundel of the 'Battersea Shield' found in the River Thames at Battersea in London, and now in the British Museum in London. Dating from *c.*350–50 BC, this copper-alloy shield cover is decorated with graceful, swirling designs and inset with red glass. It was originally fixed to a wooden shield board and would have been used in rituals or carried on parade, or perhaps was always intended as a votive offering. (Werner Forman/ Universal Images Group/Getty Images)

Yet the Roman soldiers were eager to engage. Agricola further encouraged his men with an inspiring speech before leading them out of their camp. He left the legionary infantry in front of the rampart, where they were to form a reserve force, along with four *alae* of auxiliary cavalry. Tacitus records (*Agricola* 35) that Agricola kept the legions out of the battle because he thought that to achieve a victory over the British without spilling 'Roman' – i.e. citizen – blood would be a great honour. As we have seen in previous campaigns, however, the more flexible and mobile auxiliary infantry units, with their open-order fighting style, were more suited to combat in this kind of terrain than the 'line' infantry of the legions (Gilliver 1996: 59). Agricola advanced with 8,000 auxiliary infantry, accompanied by 3,000 cavalry. The core of this auxiliary force was made up of four cohorts of

Dating from the early 1st century AD, this is the tombstone of P. Flavoleius Cordus, a soldier of the *legio XIV Gemina*. Note the detail of the dagger and sword belts, and the method of attachment of his dagger, or *pugio*. (DeAgostini/Getty Images)

Batavians and two cohorts of Tungrians. Both the Batavians and Tungrians were recruited from communities in the Rhine valley. The Batavians in particular had distinguished themselves in many campaigns and battles in Britain, where the amphibious skills of the cavalry had proved invaluable. The Roman general was concerned by the great length of the enemy lines on the mountainside and wanted to prevent the British from assaulting his infantry from the front and sides at the same time. He ordered the auxiliaries to open their ranks and spread out. When his troops were ready, Agricola dismounted from his horse and took up a position in front of the standards (Tacitus, *Agricola* 35).

Roman soldiers advanced in silence. The auxiliaries would have found it difficult to keep their usual disciplined ranks as they marched across the marshy plain. Every step could plunge a foot into a sucking, black bog, or graze an ankle against a hard, grassy tussock. Centurions could be heard exhorting their men to maintain their formation, but all around soldiers could be seen stumbling and cursing. When the Romans came within range, elite British warriors swooped past in their chariots and flung their javelins into the front ranks. Tacitus does not record how the Romans dealt with the chariots. The auxiliary cavalry units probably dashed out onto the plain and swarmed around the closest vehicles, killing the drivers and their elite passengers. The rest of the chariots fled to safety.

Meanwhile, the infantry lines began to exchange missiles. According to Tacitus, the British courageously stood their ground as the auxiliary *hastae* hailed down. Warriors skilfully deflected the Roman spears with their long swords, or caught them on their short shields, while still managing to pelt the Romans with their own missiles. Agricola then put his faith in the Batavian and Tungrian infantry, and ordered these men to fight hand-to-hand. At about 50ft from the massed ranks of British warriors, centurions roared, and the Roman infantry charged with their long, oval shields in front of their bodies, and swords drawn. The Batavians and Tungrians had trained for this kind of combat for their entire service, and were experts at close-quarter fighting. They shoved into the British warriors with their shields, and punched with their shield bosses, so they could get so close to the Caledonians that the tribesmen did not have enough room to swing their enormous, round-tipped swords. The British in the front ranks struggled to defend themselves as the Romans crushed them against their countrymen, and stabbed their unarmoured bodies and faces with their sharply pointed swords. As the Batavians and Tungrians destroyed the British units on the plain, they were joined by the rest of the auxiliary cohorts. The infantry pushed on up the hillside (Tacitus, *Agricola* 36).

Then the auxiliary cavalry units charged. They crashed into the Caledonian ranks, spearing unarmoured tribesmen with their lances and slashing with their long-bladed *spathae*. At first, the British lines recoiled at the cavalry onslaught; but the warriors soon surrounded the Roman troopers, trapping them in the infantry mêlée. Many horses lost their footing on the boggy ground and fell, spilling horsemen into the mud where they were instantly set upon. One of the first to fall was Aulus Atticus, a young prefect of a cohort whose courage and fiery horse had propelled him into the British ranks (Tacitus, *Agricola* 37). Soon, riderless horses and abandoned chariots were barrelling into both sides, the screaming and whinnying animals rearing up and trampling anyone in their path.

Many of the Caledonians remained high on the mountainside. They had a clear view of the battle and, not yet having had the chance to engage, many sneered at the smaller Roman force below. They were sure their vast numbers would quickly crush the Roman advance. Long lines of warriors began to descend the slopes and slowly moved around the side of the Roman auxiliaries, attempting to engulf them from the rear. Agricola had anticipated this, however, and he ordered the four *alae* of cavalry that he had held in reserve to block the descending tribesmen. Hundreds of elite Roman cavalrymen galloped up across the plain and swung around the infantry cohorts in a huge arc, before smashing into the Caledonian reinforcements. The ferocity of the cavalry charge stopped the British counter-attack before it had even begun. Agricola urged the *alae* to press on. They wheeled again, and charged the remaining British warriors from behind.

The British line broke. The Roman cavalry dispersed throughout the Caledonian ranks, scattering the tribesmen in all directions. Across the plain small groups of warriors tried to hold off the horsemen, while others turned to flee, only to be speared or cut down as they ran. A few unarmed warriors deliberately exposed themselves to the slash of a Roman blade. The cavalry pursuit was merciless. Some troopers took prisoners, only to butcher them so they could continue the slaughter. They chased the British tribesmen away from the battlefield, into the surrounding forest, where groups of warriors banded together and turned to ambush their pursuers.

Agricola stopped the cavalry rout. He ordered the auxiliary infantry to line out around the forests, as though they were forming a cordon during a hunt. The cavalry searched the forest clearings, while others dismounted and cautiously combed the dense thickets for hiding tribesmen. When the British saw the determined and disciplined Roman soldiers methodically sweeping through the woods, they turned, and melted away into the gathering darkness. The Romans had also had enough. They had killed 10,000 Caledonian tribesmen for the loss of only 360 of their own men (Tacitus, *Agricola* 37) and now returned to their marching camp to spend the night celebrating their long-awaited victory.

The Caledonian horde dispersed. Tribesmen fled alone or in small groups back to their farms and villages. Tacitus records (*Agricola* 38) that many burned their homes and disappeared into the wilderness, and some even turned their weapons on their own families to save them from Roman slavery. Agricola's scouts pursued a number of tribesmen, but it was clear that there was to be no attempt by the Caledonians to rally for another battle. Agricola had completed the Roman conquest of Britain. He sent the Roman fleet to sail around the whole of the north of the island to terrify the inhabitants of even the most remote parts of the territory. Autumn was fast approaching and he marched his victorious army slowly back to their winter quarters, taking a roundabout route to intimidate as many of the vanquished population as possible.

Roman short sword (*gladius*) and copper-alloy scabbard fittings. The shape of the blade of this sword is known as a 'Pompeii' type and has straight sides, and a short, triangular point. Swords of this type are the most commonly found from the second half of the 1st century AD, and replaced the 'Mainz' type, which had a much longer point, and sometimes a 'waisted' blade. (© Royal Armouries IX.5583)

Analysis

The three battles explored in the previous chapters all ended in Roman victory. Yet the Romans suffered damaging losses in the low-level conflict that persisted throughout the period covered by this book. It is worth considering some of the factors that contributed to the success or failure of both sides in pitched battle and the intervening guerrilla war.

USE OF TERRAIN

Terrain determines the nature of combat. In Britain, the forests, marshes, mountains, rivers, estuaries and coasts were as much an ally to the defending tribes as they were an obstacle to the invading Romans. Successive tribal leaders attempted to use the British terrain to their own strategic and tactical advantage. As we have seen, this was ultimately not often successful, as the Romans were able to overcome what initially appeared to be insuperable natural obstacles through a combination of training, discipline, superior weapons and equipment and the adaptability and special skills of their troops.

The Romans demonstrated their ability to surmount difficulties presented by the British terrain soon after the invasion in AD 43. When the survivors of the defeats of Caratacus and Togodumnus retreated over the Medway, they believed the river formed an unpassable barrier to the pursuing Roman army. The peculiar amphibious skills of the Batavian cavalry, who were able to cross immediately, enabled the Romans to prevail, however. In the same way, the Batavians followed British tribesmen across the Thames estuary a short time later (Cassius Dio, *Roman History* 60.20), and twice crossed the treacherous Menai Strait to Mona. The Roman Army was also able to deal with expanses of water through the superior use of planning, technology and the Romans' enormous logistical resources. Paulinus' construction of a flotilla of flat-bottomed boats specially designed to cope with the shallow waters of

the Menai Strait was an impressive feat of Roman engineering; the huge fleet gathered to transport Plautius' invasion force even more so. Agricola employed the Roman Navy more than any other commander. Captured Caledonian tribesmen told him how amazed they were by the sight of his fleet as it meant their hidden coastal settlements were no longer safe (Tacitus, *Agricola* 25).

Tacitus described Caratacus' excellent topographical knowledge and use of terrain in his guerrilla campaign against the Romans in what is now Wales (*Annals* 12.33). The steep-sided valley he chose for his 'final battle' appeared so much to his advantage, with its precipitous slopes protected by a river, that Scapula, the Roman commander, considered refusing to commit his troops to battle. The Romans were ultimately victorious, however, because of their training and discipline, and the quality of their equipment. The formation of a *testudo* of interlocked shields was a difficult manoeuvre that required a great deal of practice and leadership, and was only possible because of the standardized and well-made equipment carried by Roman soldiers.

Despite Tacitus' assertion (*Agricola* 35) that Agricola held the legions in reserve at Mons Graupius to preserve the lives of Roman citizen-soldiers, his deployment of auxiliary infantry units demonstrated their greater ability to fight in difficult country. Roman commanders regularly relied on the flexibility and mobility of their auxiliary troops when forced to engage an enemy on unfavourable terrain, particularly on wet, marshy or uneven ground, where heavily equipped legionaries were not able to move and fight in their usual close formations. The mixture of different types of troops in the Roman Army of the 1st century AD allowed Roman commanders to deal with almost any tactical situation, in almost any terrain (Gilliver 1996: 64).

PITCHED BATTLE VS GUERRILLA WARFARE

When the Romans invaded Britain in AD 43 the first reaction of the British tribes was not to assemble an army to meet them in battle. Instead, they fell back into the marshes and forests, intending to lure the Romans into unfavourable terrain where they could harass and ambush them (Cassius Dio, *Roman History* 60.19). When the British did attempt to confront the Romans with a concentration of warriors, they were easily defeated. This became a familiar pattern, which would be repeated for the rest of the century.

British tribes determined to resist were faced with a difficult choice. They could either withdraw into inhospitable terrain and engage the Romans in a long and bitter insurgency, hoping to persuade them that their invasion was not worth the expense of manpower and resources, or mass together and try again to achieve a victory in pitched battle. As we have seen, most tribes opted for a guerrilla campaign. The peoples of what is now Wales – the Silures, Deceangli and Ordovices – proved to be experts at this kind of warfare, as Scapula found to great military and ultimately personal cost. Tacitus records (*Annals* 12.32) that the Silures were so hostile to Roman expansion across the lower Severn that Scapula had to redeploy an entire legion to the area to help deal with their constant raids and ambushes, and the stress of the conflict led to his early death.

Conversely, Caratacus clearly felt that the only way to force the Roman Army out was to overcome them in battle. This was a mistake, just as it would be for the Caledonians. It was also an error for Roman commanders to believe that victory on the battlefield would end indigenous resistance. Scapula likely assumed that the defeat and capture of Caratacus would stop the Silures' insurrection; but in fact it gained little. The Romans continued to suffer loss after loss in the forests of the Welsh valleys, and successive governors were forced to devote years of campaigning, thousands of troops and enormous financial resources in an effort to bring the territory under imperial control. The fact that this was ultimately achieved proved the Roman Empire's determination to do so, and that the region's mineral resources were worth such a great cost. Unfortunately for the British tribes in what is now Wales, the Romans' eventual victory proved that neither opting for a pitched battle nor a protracted insurgency was a successful strategy.

EQUIPMENT AND FIGHTING STYLE

The Celts were skilful metalworkers. There are many examples of their decorated shields, helmets and other objects in museums around the world, which are as technically impressive as they are beautiful. The Celts also produced very effective combat armour – the helmets worn by Roman soldiers were ultimately derived from Celtic designs, as was the mail armour – yet most warriors fought with only a shield for protection, and as many sources record, often entered battle completely naked.

Panel from the 'Gundestrup Cauldron' showing mounted Celtic warriors and foot soldiers, some of whom are blowing *carnyces*. Note the helmets with crests in the shape of birds and animals, like those described by the Greek historian Diodorus Siculus (*Library of History* 5.30). An example of a helmet with a bird-shaped crest has been found in Romania. (DEA/A. DAGLI ORTI/ Getty Images)

Celtic combat was tempered by ritual and convention. As the opposing sides drew near, they attempted to intimidate each other with incredible noise: by shouting, banging their weapons and blowing their *carnyces*. Elite warriors would then step forward and boast of their achievements and challenge one another to single combat, as both armies remained in their own lines and watched the spectacle. In many cases, the victor would be decided by a combination of the volume of 'war din', the impressiveness of their warriors' bombastic performance and a few individual contests. For this kind of ritualized combat, effective body armour and helmets were not just unnecessary, they were deliberately rejected. A naked warrior proved his bravery immediately, and to overcome an armoured opponent while unprotected oneself was an impressive feat. When Celtic tribes did engage in actual battle, their weapons suited an individual fighting style. They used long swords with small points that were designed to cut and slash, and long-headed spears with long handles. Warriors needed plenty of space to wield these weapons effectively, but they also functioned as a means to keep their opponents at a distance, so that individual acts of valour were more visible.

Roman arms and armour and fighting styles were very different. A legionary soldier fought encased in flexible iron armour, with a metal helmet that covered the entire head and neck apart from the ears, eyes and mouth. He carried a large, curved, rectangular shield that covered much of his body, and fought in close cooperation with the other soldiers in his unit. The legionaries' *gladius* was famously short and designed for stabbing. A Roman soldier had to get very close to an enemy to use this weapon to any effect. This combination of armour, shield and short sword had developed over many decades as a counter to the Celts' long, slashing swords and relatively open fighting style. In pitched battle, the Romans shoved the front ranks of Celtic warriors back into their lines, forcing them together so that they were unable to swing their weapons, and where their unprotected bodies were easily pierced with the points of Roman short swords. This is why the British Celts were so quickly defeated when they attempted to meet the Roman Army in battle on open ground. On unfavourable terrain, where the legionaries' equipment and tactics could put them at a severe disadvantage against Celtic warriors, Roman commanders could deploy the mobile and flexible auxiliary units, whose arms and armour more closely matched those of the Celts, and were better suited to skirmishing and combat with a dispersed enemy.

Aftermath

An aerial view of the excavated remains of the Roman fort at Vindolanda, near Hexham in Northumberland. Several forts were built on this site; these stone foundations are the remains of buildings and defensive walls built in the 3rd and 4th centuries AD. Earlier forts were built of timber. The first fort at Vindolanda was built *c*.AD 85 by the *cohors I Tungrorum*, part of the earliest military garrison defending the new Roman frontier between the estuaries of the Tyne and Solway and likely to have been one of the cohorts that Tacitus records (*Agricola* 36) were present at the battle of Mons Graupius in AD 83. In about AD 97, this Tungrian unit was replaced by the *cohors IX Batavorum*, also probably at Mons Graupius. After building a new, larger fort, the Batavians remained at Vindolanda until *c*.AD 105, when the Tungrians appear to have returned. (English Heritage/Heritage Images/Getty Images)

Agricola left the province of Britannia in AD 84. He returned to Rome where the emperor Domitian (r. AD 81–96) awarded him an honorary triumph, and erected a public statue. Domitian tried to appoint him to the governorship of another province, but Agricola opted instead for a quiet retirement and died in AD 93 (Tacitus, *Agricola* 39–44). Soon after the battle of Mons Graupius the Caledonian tribes returned to their guerrilla campaign against the Roman Army, just as the Silures had done in the years following Scapula's victory over Caratacus. They had learnt their lesson, and never again attempted to challenge the Romans in pitched battle.

The Romans withdrew from what is now Scotland only a few years after Agricola's recall. Governing such a vast territory, with a widely dispersed

Excavated ruins of the Roman fort at Vindolanda. The unique anaerobic conditions in the soil at Vindolanda have preserved a wealth of organic remains, including the now-famous wooden writing tablets. A unit-strength report for the *cohors I Tungrorum*, compiled for the commanding officer Iulius Verecundus at some point in AD 92–97, reveals that the total number of soldiers in the cohort at that time was 752, including six centurions. Only 296 of those men were present in the garrison of the fort. The remainder had been dispatched on various duties: 337 were at Coria (Corbridge), a nearby fort where they may have been sent to reinforce another unit in preparation for a campaign against hostile British tribes; 46 were serving in the guard of the governor; one centurion was alone in Londinium (London), perhaps delivering a sensitive message; and three small detachments of six, nine and 11 men were stationed in unknown locations (the writing on the tablet is not legible), which may have been guard duty in small outposts. Around 10 per cent of the troops still at Vindolanda were unfit for duty: 15 were 'sick', six were 'wounded' and ten were suffering from 'inflammation of the eyes' (Bowman & Thomas 1991). (DEA/S. VANNINI/ Getty Images)

and still largely hostile population required a huge commitment of troops and resources, and Domitian had military ambitions elsewhere. A legion was redeployed away from Britannia, leaving only three to secure the whole province, and the Roman Army pulled back to a new frontier further south. The occupying forces built a series of forts along a military road that stretched east to west across the country from Arbeia (South Shields) on the banks of the estuary of the River Tyne to Luguvalium (Carlisle) on the Solway Firth. The military infrastructure built to support Agricola's northern campaigns was abandoned. A large legionary fortress constructed by his troops at Inchtuthil north of the Taus (River Tay) was systematically demolished and the materials destroyed. Even the hundreds of thousands of iron nails used to construct the timber fortification were collected together and buried, presumably to prevent indigenous tribes from re-using the metal.

We know little about events in the rest of Britannia for the next 25 years. Unlike the four decades following the invasion, for which we have the accounts of Cassius Dio and Tacitus, there is no surviving literary source. It is not even known who succeeded Agricola as governor. We have, however, been given a rare glimpse of military life on the frontier in this period through the discovery of the 'Vindolanda tablets'. These documents, handwritten in ink on small pieces of wood, include unit strength reports, accounts, lists, and a whole host of official military and personal correspondence relating to the Roman fort at Vindolanda, which was built near modern-day Hexham in Northumberland. Many of the tablets were written while the *cohors IX Batavorum* was stationed at Vindolanda. The unit's prefect, Flavius Cerialis, features in much of the surviving correspondence, along with his wife Sulpicia Lepidina.

A surviving tablet from the early AD 90s documents the number of soldiers involved in different building projects at the fort; 12 were helping to construct a bathhouse, suggesting that auxiliary soldiers, despite their varied origins, quickly adopted 'Roman' practices (Haynes 2013: 171–75). Unfortunately, the tablets contain little description of the British people who lived around the fort, or the

This wooden writing tablet from Vindolanda, dated to c.AD 90–105, is a birthday-party invitation sent to Sulpicia Lepidina, wife of Flavius Cerialis, prefect of the *cohors IX Batavorum* from Claudia Severa, who was the wife of another officer, Aelius Brocchus. The auxiliary soldiers at Vindolanda embraced Roman foodstuffs, such as wine, *garum* (a kind of fermented fish sauce) and olive oil. The tablets record a wide range of other foods at the fort, including wheat, barley, beans, poultry, venison, honey and spices such as cumin (De la Bédoyère 2013: 168), but also show that the auxiliaries brought some of their own dining customs with them to Britain. Unlike legionaries, who drank a kind of soured wine, the Batavians and Tungrians drank beer. One tablet contains a reference to a 'brewer' working at the fort, and in another, a decurion wrote to the commanding officer of the *cohors IX Batavorum* asking for more beer for his men as they had run out (Haynes 2013: 180). (CM Dixon/Print Collector/ Getty Images)

soldiers' relationship with them. A fragment of what appears to be a military intelligence report informs its recipient that the Britons are 'naked' (or perhaps 'unprotected by armour') and there are many cavalry. We also learn that the cavalry do not carry swords and they do not mount to throw their javelins. The report's author uses the derogative term *Brittunculi* ('wretched little Britons') to describe the British horsemen. If nothing else, this tells us something of the Roman soldiers' attitude to the indigenous population.

It is a very rare privilege for historians to have access to such documents. Excavations at the fort are ongoing, and the archive of translated and published tablets continues to grow. Through them we can get closer than historians previously believed possible to understanding what life was really like for Roman soldiers serving in Britain, or indeed anywhere in the Roman Empire.

Display of leather footwear excavated at Vindolanda. Preserved in the wet, anaerobic soil, more than 5,000 leather shoes have been found so far; many belonged to women and children, showing that many soldiers' families and other civilians lived at the fort. (Andre Poling/ullstein bild via Getty Images)

BIBLIOGRAPHY

Ancient sources

Born in Bithynia in Asia Minor, **Cassius Dio** (*c*.AD 150–*c*.235) served as a Roman senator, twice as consul and as governor of provinces in Asia, Africa and Pannonia. Dio wrote an enormous history of the Roman Empire in Greek, which stretched from the founding of Rome until AD 229, in 80 books. Only part of this work survives, much of it preserved in the writings of later historians. Book 60 contains the sole surviving literary account of the invasion of Britain, and Book 62 one of only three accounts of the rebellion of Boudicca.

Diodorus Siculus (*c*.AD 20–*c*.80), a Greek historian from Sicily, wrote a 40-volume history of the world from the mythical past up to 54 BC, which he called a *Library of History*. As the title implies, Diodorus used many sources, often copying them so closely that historians have been able to reconstruct parts of their work through his. Book 5 contains a detailed description of the Celts, including their personal appearance, clothing, weapons and way of fighting.

Herodian (born *c*.AD 179) wrote a history of the Roman Empire in Greek from the death of the emperor Marcus Aurelius in AD 180 to the beginning of the reign of Gordian III in AD 238, events which he recorded as having taken place within his own lifetime. Very little is known about him but, unlike most Roman historians, he was probably of relatively low birth and only held a minor official position in the empire. Herodian lived through and described a very turbulent period in Roman history, which he recorded in his *History of the Roman Empire* in eight books. Book 3 contains an account of the campaigns of the emperor Septimius Severus (r. AD 193–211) in northern Britain in AD 208.

Julius Caesar (*c*.102–44 BC) was a Roman statesman and politician and arguably Rome's most talented military commander. After leading his own army in the conquest of Gaul, he made two expeditions to Britain in 55 BC and 54 BC.

Caesar's victory against the forces of Pompey the Great (106–48 BC) in the civil war of 49–48 BC left him in sole control of the Roman Empire, which he ruled as *dictator* until his assassination in 44 BC. Caesar's accounts of his own exploits in the conquest of Gaul and the civil war of 49–48 BC are clear, concise and completely devoid of rhetoric. Books 4 and 5 of the *Gallic Wars* contain accounts of his British expeditions, and Book 6 contains a description of Celtic society and religion, including the role of the druids.

Marcus Annaeus Lucanus (AD 39–65), known as **Lucan**, was a Roman poet. Lucan's family was prominent in Rome and he was a close friend of the emperor Nero (r. AD 54–68) under whose patronage he became quite well known. At some point Lucan and Nero feuded, though there are conflicting accounts of the cause. In AD 65 Lucan became involved in a plot against Nero. When the conspiracy was uncovered, Lucan chose to commit suicide and died aged only 25. His most famous work, the *Pharsalia*, is an epic poem that narrates the events of the civil war between Caesar and Pompey in 49–48 BC.

Polybius (*c*.200–118 BC) was a politician and soldier from Megalopolis in Greece and an important figure in the Achaean League, which governed much of the Peloponnese. In 167 BC he was transported to Rome as a political prisoner, where he became a close friend of the Roman statesman and general Scipio Aemilianus (185–128 BC), also known as Scipio Africanus the Younger, who he accompanied to North Africa during the Third Punic War (149–146 BC). Polybius witnessed the destruction of Carthage in 148 BC, which took place the same year that Greece fell under Roman control. Polybius wrote a 40-volume history of the Mediterranean from 220 BC to 146 BC in which he attempted to explain to a Greek audience how Rome had created its vast empire. Only the first five books of Polybius' *Histories* have been preserved complete, but many parts of the other books survive in fragments. Book 2 contains accounts of Roman campaigns against Celtic tribes, including a vivid description of the battle of Telamon in 225 BC.

Hailing from Pontus in Asia Minor, the Greek scholar **Strabo** (*c*.64–*c*.25 BC) travelled widely and visited much of Asia Minor, Greece, Egypt and Italy. He studied in Rome and Alexandria and wrote books on history and geography. Only his *Geography* has survived, in 17 books, which contains detailed descriptions of the different regions of the Roman world. Book 4 describes Gaul and Britain.

Writing in Latin, Publius Cornelius **Tacitus** (*c*.AD 57–*c*.117) was one of the most important Roman historians. He was born in southern Gaul (modern Provence) but moved to Rome and entered public life. He served as a senator and held a number of offices, including the consulship in AD 97. Tacitus was married to the daughter of Gnaeus Julius Agricola, governor of the Roman province of Britannia AD 77–84, and Tacitus probably served under his father-in-law as a military tribune for at least part of this period. Tacitus wrote a biography of Agricola in AD 98, in which he described the governor's achievements in Britain, and in particular his campaigns against the Caledonian tribes in the north of the island. He also wrote a detailed description of the German tribes, the *Germania*, and two major works of history known as the *Annals of Imperial Rome* and the *Histories*. The *Annals* covers the period AD 14–68, and provides much of the surviving evidence for events in Britain in the decades following the Roman invasion in AD 43.

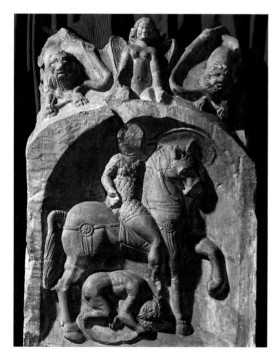

Detail from a funerary stele erected in honour of a Thracian cavalryman called Longinus Spadezematygus, found outside the walls of the veteran colony at Camulodunum (modern-day Colchester). Longinus was a *duplicarius* (literally 'double pay man', a junior officer below a decurion) in the *ala Thracum*, who was born near Sofia in modern-day Bulgaria. His two-part name, which combines common Roman and native elements, shows how auxiliary soldiers often adopted Roman names on enlistment. Longinus is wearing a *lorica squamata*, and the detail of his horse's tack can be seen clearly. He has ridden down a naked British warrior. (DEA PICTURE LIBRARY/Getty Images)

Primary sources

Cassius Dio, trans. E. Cary (1924). *Roman History Vol. VII*. Harvard, MA: Harvard University Press. https://penelope.uchicago.edu/Thayer/E/Roman/Texts/Cassius_Dio/home.html

Diodorus Siculus, trans. C. Oldfather (1939). *Library of History Vol. III*. Harvard, MA: Harvard University Press. https://penelope.uchicago.edu/Thayer/E/Roman/Texts/Diodorus_Siculus/home.html

Herodian, trans. E.C. Echols (1961). *Herodian of Antioch's History of the Roman Empire*. Berkeley & Los Angeles, CA: University of California Press. https://www.livius.org/sources/content/herodian-s-roman-history/herodian

Julius Caesar, trans. C. Hammond (1996). *The Gallic War*. Oxford: Oxford University Press.

Lucan, trans. S. Braund (1992). *Civil War*. Oxford: Oxford University Press.

Polybius, trans. R. Waterfield (2010). *The Histories*. Oxford: Oxford University Press.

Tacitus, trans. M. Grant (1959). *The Annals of Imperial Rome*. Harmondsworth: Penguin.

Tacitus, trans. A. Birley (1999). *Agricola and Germania*. Oxford: Oxford University Press.

Tacitus, trans. C. Moore (1925). *Histories*. Harvard, MA: Harvard University Press. https://penelope.uchicago.edu/Thayer/E/Roman/Texts/Tacitus/home.html

Secondary sources

Aldhouse-Green, M. (2010). *Caesar's Druids: Story of an Ancient Priesthood*. New Haven, CT & London: Yale University Press.

Anders, A. (2015). 'The face of Roman Skirmishing', *Historia: Zeitschrift für Alte Geschichte* 64.3: 263–300.

Birley, A. (2018). *Vindolanda Guide*. Vindolanda Trust.

Birley, A.R., Birley, A. & de Bernardo Stempel, P. (2013). 'A Dedication by the "Cohors I Tungrorum" at Vindolanda to a Hitherto Unknown Goddess', *Zeitschrift für Papyrologie und Epigraphik* 186: 287–300.

Bishop, M.C. & Coulston, J.C.N (2006). *Roman Military Equipment: From the Punic Wars to the Fall of Rome*. 2nd Edition. Oxford: Oxbow Books.

Bowman, A. & Thomas, D. (1991). 'A Military Strength Report from Vindolanda', *The Journal of Roman Studies* 81: 62–73.

Buckland, P. (1978). 'A First-Century Shield from Doncaster, Yorkshire', *Britannia* 9: 247–69.

Campbell, D.B. (2010). *Mons Graupius AD 83: Rome's battle at the edge of the world*. Campaign 224. Oxford: Osprey Publishing.

Campbell, D.B. (2015). 'A Note on the Battle of Mons Graupius', *The Classical Quarterly* 65.1: 407–10.

Connolly, P. (2016). *Greece and Rome at War*. Barnsley: Frontline (first published in 1981).

Cuff, D. (2011). 'The King of the Batavians: Remarks on Tab. Vindol. III, 628', *Britannia* 42: 145–56.

Cunliffe, P. (1997). *The Ancient Celts*. Oxford: Oxford University Press.

De La Bédoyère, G. (2003). *Defying Rome: The Rebels of Roman Britain*. Stroud: Tempus.

De La Bédoyère, G. (2013). *Roman Britain: A New History*. London: Thames and Hudson.

Dudley, D. & Webster, G. (1962). *The Rebellion of Boudicca*. London: Routledge & Kegan Paul.

Fraser, J. (2008). *The Roman Conquest of Scotland: The Battle of Mons Graupius AD 84*. Stroud: The History Press (first published in 2005).

Gilliver, C. (1996). 'Mons Graupius and the Role of Auxiliaries in Battle', *Greece & Rome* 43.1: 54–67.

Goldsworthy, A. (2011). *The Complete Roman Army*. London: Thames & Hudson (first published in 2003).

Hassall, M.W.C. (1970). 'Batavians and the Roman Conquest of Britain', *Britannia* 1: 131–36.

Haynes, I. (2013). *Blood of the Provinces: The Roman Auxilia and the Making of Provincial Society from Augustus to the Severans*. Oxford: Oxford University Press.

MacMullen, R. (1984). 'The Legion as a Society', *Historia: Zeitschrift für Alte Geschichte* 33.4: 440–56.

Pollard, N. & Berry, J. (2015). *The Complete Roman Legions*. London: Thames & Hudson (first published in 2012).

Prendergast, E. & Lucas, A.T. (1962). 'National Museum of Ireland Archaeological Acquisitions in the Year 1960', *The Journal of the Royal Society of Antiquaries of Ireland* 92.2: 139–73.

Rowlett, R. (1993). 'North Gaulish Forms on the Gundestrup Cauldron', *Proceedings of the Harvard Celtic Colloquium* 13: 166–82.

Sabin, P. (2000). 'The Face of Roman Battle', *The Journal of Roman Studies* 90: 1–17.

Speidel, M. (1991). 'Swimming the Danube under Hadrian's eyes: a feat of the Emperor's Batavi horse guard', *Ancient Society* 22: 277–82.

St Joseph, J.K. (1978). 'The Camp at Durno, Aberdeenshire, and the Site of Mons Graupius', *Britannia* 9: 71–87.

Taylor, T. (1992). 'The Gundestrup Cauldron', *Scientific American* 266.3: 84–89.

Van Driel-Murray, C. (2001). 'Vindolanda and the Dating of Roman Footwear', *Britannia* 32: 185–97.

Webster, G. (1980). *The Roman Invasion of Britain*. London: Batsford.

Webster, G. (1981). *Rome Against Caratacus: The Roman Campaigns in Britain AD 48–58*. London: Batsford.

Plaque from a diploma granting citizenship to a Roman auxiliary soldier and his descendants, issued during the reign of the emperor Domitian. (DeAgostini/Getty Images)

INDEX

References to illustrations are shown in **bold**.
References to plates are shown in bold with
caption pages in brackets, e.g. **42–43**, (44).